First published in London, 2021 by Dog Section Press,
a worker-owned cooperative

Printed by Calverts Ltd., a worker-owned cooperative

ISBN 9781916036581
Published under Creative Commons Attribution-NonCommercial
4.0 International Public Licence

Book design by Matt Bonner • revoltdesign.org
Dog Section Press logo by Marco Bevilacqua

POST-INTERNET FAR RIGHT

Fascism in the age of the internet

By
12 RULES FOR WHAT

Illustrated by
WANT SOME STUDIO

CONTENTS

———

AUTHORS' NOTE

———

This book is meant to be provisional, combative, and, we hope, insightful. It is also a fairly short book, and therefore necessarily incomplete. You are very welcome, once you've read it, to offer comments, thoughts and feedback – our contact details are on the last page.

Thank you to our editors, proofreaders, discussants, friends, families and comrades.

DEDICATION

———

Anti-fascist history is a sea of a billion anonymous acts. This book, like all mere writing, is a tiny wavelet surrounded by great waves of astonishing heroism. It is dedicated to them.

INTRODUCTION

The far right has changed. Since the rise of the internet, it has scattered, diversified, and stuck itself back together. The internet has facilitated these tendencies, filtering and contorting familiar forms of activity and ideology, and pushed far-right groups to adapt, causing the decline of some formations and the break-up of others. But the far right has not gone away – far from it – it is more powerful now than it has been for a generation. It has produced new configurations of tactics, priorities, and goals. Those who have survived the arrival of the internet have found a greater capacity to exert power than at any point since the Second World War.

These changes are still little understood, either in the popular consciousness or in left-wing movements. Conceptions that focus on Nazism or skinheads or attempt to label groups only in terms of their policy platform, or describe all forms of political authoritarianism as 'fascist', are not only inaccurate but counter-productive. The types of far-right thought and action developing in the wake of the internet are much more varied and complex than these labels seem to indicate, and the type of thought and action that will predominate in the long-run has yet to be settled. The far right is in a state of productive diversification. It has yet to cohere around a new stable formulation; however, it almost certainly will, and we must be ready for it.

To interrupt these new formations, we must recognise both the particularity of the threat and its variety. It would be a disaster if the far right's opponents were not to update their models, and either find fascism everywhere they looked, or instead find nothing worthy of a response. In our heightened moment, perhaps the latter seems unlikely. However, both underestimating and misunderstanding the threat remain real possibilities, because, as we will discuss in our final few chapters, the far right is perfectly capable of wrapping its ideas – even those that lead to genocide – in ostensibly innocuous positions.

The far right has risen and intensified in the last few years because it can put certain forms of masculinity to work, forms which can be summarised as 'the fantasy of martial life' (chapter 1). The emotions that feed this fantasy can be stimulated online to promote far-right ideas (chapter 2), produce confusion and mistrust (3), and galvanize political action. The various political forms this takes – far-right influencers and their audiences (4), right-wing intellectuals (5), street movements (6), membership organisations that attempt to integrate these various parts (7), spree shooters (8), and so on – are in tension with one another.

Particularly, there is a tension between movement-building and deadly violence, or fascism in its 'identitarian' form and 'blackpilled' neo-Nazism. But this tension is not eternal. And the conditions under which these two halves might come back together are now also emerging, in the form of an 'ecofascist' politics that utilises global climate breakdown to justify murder (9). This 'ecofascism' is not a homogenous movement, nor can it be, for it contains contradictory ideas of its own. Particularly, it will struggle to articulate the contradictions between ecology, ethnonationalism, and economic imperatives, like its historical forebears did. These contradictions are handles that anti-fascists can grasp to destroy it, but the scale and tactics of anti-fascism must be rethought (this book's conclusion).

This is a lot for one book, but the scope is deliberate and reflects the multiplicity of movements, message boards, slogans, thoughts, platforms, tendencies, acts of violence, strategic concealments, shitposts, stunts, and parties that make up the 'post-internet far right'. Rather than merely explain the underlying ideas or the structures of particular groups or their new public faces, we've chosen to cover all of these dimensions at once, to give an account we hope is both theoretically rich and attentive to the actions of real people doing real things. In some sense, the argument of the book is identical with its structure: the rising articulations of far-right politics that take place through chapters 2-5 on 'metapolitics', their arrival in physical space in chapter 6, their organisation into coherent political groups in chapter 7, and their strategic antagonism with the terrorists in chapter 8 *is* the structure of how a movement composes itself.

———————

None of these elements is wholly new. Classical fascist parties fed off the militarist forms of masculine subjectivity that spewed from the First World War. The far right has long tried to spread its ideas metapolitically – the idea that "politics is downstream of culture."[1] From the European New Right, 'metapolitics' became an explicit strategy, but the use of conspiracy and propaganda stretches back much further. It has also always had its conspicuous individuals and ideologues, whose functions have ranged from absolute dictators to idealised victims, and who have often existed in tension with the masses who support them. There have been many attempts in the last 150 years to make a respectable intellectual community of far-right thinkers. From these disparate parts, the far right has assembled many different kinds of organisation, and the use of terrorist violence stretches back through the entire history of the movement. Recognisably modern forms of non-state far-right terrorism are visible in Reconstruction Era murders by the Ku Klux Klan. The far right has also long been concerned with the environment, although with concerns that are often very different from their left-wing counterparts.

But all these aspects have been transformed by the rise of the internet.

Masculinity has changed. The possibilities for forming male space have increased online while they have decreased IRL, and new forms of masculinity have come to the fore, variously reviled and celebrated by the far right.

Metapolitics has become politics' default. The internet's uneven texture — vast savannahs of public videos and Medium posts give way to encrypted Discord servers, where invite-only groups plot in secret, or a mislabeled link leads suddenly into ugly panels of high-turnover anonymous imageboards — has meant the proliferation of forms of digital partitioning, both transparently aggressive and as disinterested as mathematics, contorting the distribution of the public and private realms almost beyond recognition. All the internet's parts are *in principle* linkable. Port-holes can open up at any time; the online world is like the physical world would be if all distances were merely statistical. Such a statistical way of encountering reality has allowed conspiracy to move from a fringe activity to the mainstream and for political ideas to circulate back and forth from the fringe, gaining potency in movement. While this was neither planned by the far right nor does it exclusively benefit them, they have capitalised on their new ability to project their conspiratorial thinking, and the conditions of growing mistrust in traditional information sources have made fertile terrain for their messages.

Similarly, hierarchy within movements has taken on a statistical quality. The figures who now lead far-right movements have no special command over the actions of the people within them, in the quasi-military manner of classical fascist parties. Instead, they hold highly variable influence over huge numbers of people, some of whom are highly obedient to what they think the message is – which can lead to the 'scripted violence' explored in chapter 8. Regardless of commitment, many people are exposed to fascist and far-right ideas, laying the groundwork for future movements. But as yet, these far-right reactionaries produce audiences, not movements. And they, as well as their anti-fascist opponents, have benefitted from the ability to organise impromptu demonstrations that momentarily transform this audience into a fragile crowd faster through the internet, and to frame and reframe real-world action.

The right's intellectual apparatus takes in a huge number of disparate, indeed conflicting, parts. Now it incorporates the thinkers of right-accelerationism, neo-reaction and the human-biodiversity movement, as well as more conventional technological authoritarians, gender reactionaries, and ethnonationalists. These are diverse ideas, but commonly aspire to give far-right movements the appearance of an intellectual heft they do not really possess.

In Europe, identitarianism has emerged as the predominant form of fascist organising within membership organisations, as national movements take on a more parochial character in the context of pan-European organising online. Although the process had already begun before it became an online phenomenon, the internet has undoubtedly accelerated the transformation from cell-based terrorist groups to 'stochastic terrorism'. Pronounced tensions exist between these figures and the more formal organisations.

As noted above, these tensions might continue forever were it not for one thing: the overwhelming magnitude of the coming climate breakdown. 'Ecofascism' draws on the long history of connection between the far right and environmentalism, but has been given new life on the internet – not only as the far right come to accept the reality of climate breakdown but also as a way to combine incompatible racist and misanthropic positions, spurred on by the spectacle of disaster that the internet circulates. It is also structured around fundamental contradictions in far-right and fascist thinking.

―――――――

We name this grouping the 'post-internet far right'. The 'post-internet' is not a time *after* the internet, but a time in which the internet has receded into the background of how life appears *simply to be*. It is no longer remarkable that politics is mediated through the internet. The 'far right' of the title consists of widely diverging groups, movements, and interests; however, threading them all together is racism in its various forms and reactionary gender politics. These exist on a spectrum, from the racism and misogyny of the street-based far right to 'blackpilled' fantasies of mass murder. How have each of these groups, meditated now through the internet, transformed?

In the UK, the most prominent form of racism on the far right continues to be Islamophobia, present across the political spectrum in one form or another, but intensifying on the conservative right, among far-right civic nationalist street movements, through the identitarian movement, and onwards into ethnonationalism. Widespread, it comes in many forms: hatred of Muslims spurred by the fear of terrorism, the association of Islam with sexual violence, and the fear of changing demographics, with Muslims imagined as a growing population who will come to 'replace' whites. These three variants of Islamophobia are associated with increasingly extreme far-right groups, and increasingly totalising conspiracies among them.

Less publicly expressed – until the mid-2020 Black Lives Matter uprising – were antisemitism and anti-Black racism. Once the central forms of far-right racism (along with the archaic-seeming anti-Catholicism, anti-Irish racism in the UK, and anti-Freemasonry in the US), they nevertheless continued to inspire violence from racists across society, and in the case of anti-Black racism, the state.

Antisemitic politics and its conspiratorial derivatives are endemic to the far right, as we will show in our chapter on conspiracy theories, but it is infrequently the public dogma of contemporary far-right groups. When it is, it often marks a more generally extreme position. National Action, a UK-based neo-Nazi group whose members have called for the killings of Jews and Black people, is one such case. Slightly to their left, Generation Identity, a far-right group with a slicker version of white nationalism at its core, prevents those who bring up 'the Jewish Question' from joining. However, antisemitism is growing again on the far right.

Likewise, anti-Black racism is increasingly prominent in the more extreme parts of the far right. The space in which the far right and the state combine most obviously, anti-Black racism, has several fixations online: the relation between race and IQ and 'interracial crime', as well as support for vigilante murderers and the killing of black people by police. In the year before the publication of this book, anti-Black racism became once again a central feature of far-right racism.

These different forms of racism have different places in the far right. The threat from black people that the far right hallucinates is a slow-burning degrading of social order, rather than its absolute termination (Islamophobia) or its endless manipulation (antisemitism).

Misogyny is an integral part of each of these forms of racism, and we will detail the transformation from misogyny to racism (and *vice versa*) at length in the first chapter. From the Democratic Football Lads Alliance's (DFLA) marches against 'grooming gangs', which mobilised a combination of racist and sexist sentiments, to the posters in neo-Nazi groups, who gloried in racist and violently misogynistic content on Telegram, the intertwining of gendered and racist hatred has intensified.

We want to make several further points about the way this book is structured.

The first point is about scope. We're writing almost exclusively about people on the far right who write and speak in English. This might, in the past, have severely restricted the range of movements and forms it was possible to cover. Writers not conversant with many different languages (which includes us) were left to generalise about other national far-rights, a problem that often led to distortions and caricatures of what were highly divergent national political tendencies. This is still a problem, but less so. Thanks to the anglicising tendencies of the internet, 'anglophones' no longer means only native speakers. Martin Sellner, the Austrian *de facto* leader of the pan-European Generation Identity, who daubed swastikas on synagogues as a teenager, speaks excellent English. International (anglophone) communication is a vector of the transformation of the far right in recent years. Nevertheless, pronounced weaknesses remain in our ability to cover all the important parts of what is a global movement. The German, Brazilian and Indian far rights are, in particular, under-explored and we would welcome attempts to expand or critique the framework proffered here in these directions.

The second point is about terms. There is perhaps no term more fraught in political theory than 'fascism'. George

Orwell, who died in 1950, claimed it had, already in his time, become a simple slur. And it undoubtedly has that function today. However, we are not academics: terminology, we think, is not merely a matter of conceptual distinction. It is also a matter of force. 'Fascism' often *is* just a slur; sometimes slurs are useful. More generally, there is not always time to make fine distinctions. But it is not always an accurate slur, and 'fascist!' has lost much of its force. One theory of historical memory goes: looking in our rear-view mirror, we can only see with any great clarity 'the last hill'. Behind that, even great mountains can be obscured. The mid-20th century struggle against fascism is one such mountain, but in 2021 there are already many hills in the way. This forgetting makes calling 'fascist!' less effective; it also makes it easier for fascism to form. We have therefore reserved the term 'fascism' for particular, totalising movements that organise in quasi-paramilitary ways for the construction of an ethnostate. We also use it, on occasion, to name the purified, supposedly coherent form of a particular ideology, as in the chapter on 'Fascist feelings'.

We distinguish between conservatism, reactionary politics, and fascism.[2] The distinction rests on how far these three different movements are willing to go in the defence of the *status quo*. Conservatives are content to manage the transformation of existing social relations. Reactionaries want the resumption of past social relations. Fascists are looking for the complete revolution of society. Fascists have wider aims and use more drastic means to accomplish them than do reactionaries and their sense of the space of politics is also significantly wider, so that every part of life is a moment in a generalised struggle, and every moment is a threat to order. They are concerned with the totality. Today, what is included in this 'totality' is perhaps even wider than it was in the 1930s. This is a consequence of us now being deeper into capitalism. Fascism's increasingly general conception of totality is parasitic on capitalism's increasing command of the substance of life.

'Fascism' has often been taken as the rightward limit of politics. We do not think this is so. It is necessary to add to our triptych of conservatives, reactionaries, and fascists a fourth element: the blackpilled. This tendency, which spawned the Christchurch shooter and other stochastic terrorists, has largely forgotten the ultimate ends of social transformation in their focus on brutal violence. It is sometimes known as 'accelerationism' (although this term has many other uses) or as 'SIEGEpilled', a reference to the terrorist propagandising of James Mason. These would-be murderers plan to start a race war. Although, for some, there is an image of a new world beyond it, for most, the war itself is the principle fixation.

There are other ways of thinking through this transformation from fascism to 'blackpilled'. The relationship between means and ends transforms. For conservatives, a certain set of 'means' for politics are the ultimate end: the maintenance of the current arrangement of power is the purpose. For reactionaries, or the far right, the ends often justify the means. For fascists this is true as well, but there is also a glorification of political force itself (a 'means') that makes the struggle of politics itself an end. In the blackpilled, extreme violence is still a means, but it obscures or replaces the ends. Like all groups that push for always greater intensity, strange transformations of fascist ideology occur rapidly and repeatedly: aspects of wider fascist practice reach a limit and are converted into something else entirely.

What does it mean to distinguish between conservatives, reactionaries, fascists, and the blackpilled? Not only 'What do these distinctions try to display?' but 'Why would we make such distinctions when all of them are to be opposed?' This question goes to the heart of our methodology here: not a Marxist nor a liberal nor an anarchist account of the far right, but an anti-fascist one. It is an account aimed at the dissection of an enemy. We want to make clear that the far right is both a) massively diverse and b) almost completely contiguous (that is, it's possible to get from one part of it to another with relative ease). Our opposition to the far right manifests itself in an analytic style that sees it as both opposable and organised such that it could rapidly become a greater threat than it already is.

Writing about the far right on the internet has often eroticised it as perverse, strange, inexplicably vile and yet tempting. Journalistic disquisitions on 4chan are perhaps the worst offenders. One motivation of this eroticising style of writing is easy to grasp: the internet itself must be made scary, the safe path provided only by blue-check Twitter accounts and traditional news outlets. This book attempts to counter this tendency. There's nothing occult in the source code of imageboards. Indeed, the way that the far right use the internet – anonymously, or with aliases, often different and fleeting across many different platforms, with faddish engagement on new platforms and a few stable places to hang out, increasingly uninterested in the public presentation of a stable persona – is consistent with usage amongst younger people more generally. It is not the internet itself that is the bearer of fascist thought, nor is it some arcane system of technology use that makes fascists.

Let us make a small caveat. 'Affordances' are those aspects of an object, like the handle of a mug, which seem to 'offer' the user a way to engage with it. They direct our action, but can be disobeyed, and objects used 'against the grain'. In online platforms, affordances are almost comically enlarged, and almost nothing else is visible, like a huge mug handle that continually gravitates towards your hand and calls you to grab it. Thus, action flows through the use-space in a much more constrained way than the physical world. The internet, while not the bearer of fascist thought, has been designed, and could therefore also be redesigned to afford the far right less room for manoeuvre, to make forms of far-right thought and practice less 'automatic'.

It would, of course, be a mistake to regard the internet as the only – or even the principal – force transforming politics in the last ten years. Beneath and through the technical transformation is a crisis: one that began with finance but metastasised rapidly into a high-dimensional crisis of society-writ-large – governance, trust, reproduction, masculinity, health and, most generally, life on this planet. This crisis will show itself throughout in various forms. Clearly the rise of the contemporary far right is connected to it – we might even say it's *a function* of it – but the sheer complexity of the crisis makes this claim almost platitudinous. Let us simply say now, while attempting to avoid banal claims that 'everything is political', that algorithmic curation systems are intertwined with the techniques of counterinsurgency, that 'rhetorical polarisation' is a remediation of class politics, and that splintering effects in networks are indissociable from the neurotic rejection of xenoestrogens in food.

Our conclusion concerns anti-fascist movements themselves. What is their function? What is their future? It should be clear that answering this question can only be done after the proceeding analysis has been undertaken. And it is also important that anti-fascism not be taken to be a single unified thing. If there are now many different kinds of far-right or fascist politics, there are many different kinds of anti-fascism too. We want to encourage anti-fascism as an important function of all leftist organisations, and not just the preserve of specialised groups or movements. This diversification of roles means the end of exclusively black bloc, exclusively electoral, or exclusively state-sanctioned anti-fascism. The strategy discussed in the conclusion will make clear the sheer diversity of roles that a viable anti-fascist movement requires, and we hope it can spur the production of a robust ecology of anti-fascist organisations and functions.

INTRODUCTION

FASCIST FEELINGS

————

Why care about fascists' feelings? First, because that's where the radicalisation process begins. Each chapter of this book articulates a stage of the process through which feelings and emotions mutate into fully formed political movements. Without the later stages, fascist feelings might never become politically important, but without those initial feelings of inadequacy, hate, or alienation, and without their continual replenishment, the far right wouldn't have the purchase it does now. Second, although all political movements have an imaginary,[3] fascism's is particularly prominent, so prominent as to often seem like its principal driving force. This is not because fascists are particularly imaginative but because, lacking a material basis for their politics (such as class struggle or the struggles of the oppressed), fascists instead think in terms of quasi-mythic, imaginary forms — always metaphysically clashing in a realm of pure strife, its images deeply freighted with feeling. And third, it's also here that the deradicalisation process can begin, a process we will discuss in our conclusion.

Capitalism produces people – you, me, everyone you know. It works on and through all of us, moulding us into the people we become, just as we mould it. Capitalism today does not produce people like it did in the 1920s. Its requirements and possibilities have changed. The capitalist subject of neoliberalism can be characterised as 'the achievement-subject' – a self-exploiting kind of personhood, subsumed in an endless flow of images, tending nowhere in particular, but always alert to the possibility of increasing its personal value.[4] Those who do not make themselves into productive components of the general accumulation simply have not tried hard enough. Because some *must* therefore fail, failure is built-in to the production of people. Failure is treated as aberrant, but in class society, it's structural.

When something fails reliably, we can say it has a 'failure mode'. Fascism might be seen as a failure mode of capitalism. It is one of the many ways in which the underlying capitalist impulse to reproduce the conditions of accumulation might mutate and survive under crisis conditions. Similarly, we can think of a fascist as a particular failure mode of capitalist people-production. But because the capitalism of the 21st century is not like that of the 1930s, so the fascism of the 21st century will not be the same. And, likewise, the production of fascists – those who desire and build fascism – has also changed.

Perhaps the most sympathetic possible account of some fascists now is that they desire an end to the inanity of life under capitalism. As the organisation of life by capitalism ever deepens, fascism takes positions on more and more aspects of life that seemed outside the realm of politics. However, its syncretism and totalising scope exist not because of the breadth of its imagination but because of its systematisation of all the brutal techniques of discipline and social control. In this sense, fascism is capitalism's *bleeding edge*, but temporally displaced. Its regressive and reactionary content, which it presents as revolutionary, is operationalised as the doomed and violent defence of the social life liberal capitalism attempts to transform. Fascists rightly reject the order of the present, but they do so spurred on by a false view of a lost, masculine, racially homogenous past. They desire not the end of this system built on misery and brutality but the redistribution of suffering back towards nationalised, racialised and gendered Others: a radicalisation of politics that ends up affirming the most brutal – and conventional – parts of capitalism's alienating logic, but only for these Others. We will return again and again to this 'normie' radicalism, this militarised articulation of the burning core of the present.

Fascism feeds on crises. After the First World War, the crisis seemed total: military, political, social, and economic. But it was also a subjective crisis: a masculine crisis. In *Male Fantasies*, Klaus Theweleit begins with memoirs of the Freikorps.[5] Here, intimacy with women is not merely shunned: "There is more in play here than simple prudishness or questions of morality; we are dealing with the warding off of a threat."[6] Theweleit suggests something that perhaps remains true:

with far-right feelings, the warding off of a subjectively consuming sexual relationship is foundational.

But now masculine failure is more variegated. It produces diverse and complicated feelings: hatred, a passionate need for as well as a fear of intimacy, a disgust for what is uncontrollable or unfamiliar, a feeling that everything lacks potency, lacks force, a feeling that the world has been degraded, a suspicion that power is against you, a listlessness, a lack of clarity, and the feeling of being outside of the world, and a blind rage. Although this failure can be specific (for example, the failure 'to protect our girls' so potent for the Democratic Football Lads Alliance (DFLA)),[7] more often it is a broader failure to become subjectively meaningful at all.

On 4chan and other tributary cultural formations for the contemporary far right, feelings of subjective failure are ubiquitous. For most of early 4chan, 'NEETs' (Not in Education, Employment or Training – dropouts stereotypically dwelling in their parents' basements) formed the self-conceived community. Compare – bathetically – these quotidian scenes to the foundational crisis of masculinity for the Freikorps: losing the First World War. For the far right today, even failure is degraded.

The more lackadaisical the young man (and it is mostly, although not entirely, young men) becomes, the more he fails by social standards, the more he hunts for the singular pursuit, a singular strategy that will make him vital and whole. The route out of this failure finds its form also in the quotidian. Fascist narratives of overcoming are not so different from self-help literature, except they also accommodate the urge to kill and to die. They fixate on the 'non-productive' parts – the weightlifting, the personal grooming – and leave out the 'productive' parts like studying to get a better job. More importantly still, they tie the young man into a mythic community, and tell him that he is failing because of some other thing elsewhere, something to fixate on and hate. And to take his place in the mythic community, they tell him, he must be prepared to fight.

These narratives of self-improvement contain just enough death-wish, just enough self-hatred, to justify and explain the amplifying social isolation and anonymity that becoming a fascist on the internet requires. Although it's a theoretical mistake to start with the isolated individual, self-isolation almost necessarily precedes radicalisation, and the internet has created mechanisms for potential fascists to (again the rejection of intimacy) *self-isolate together.*

The project of becoming a 'true man' must be both thought and enacted. It is not enough to merely watch the news and feel hatred – although that is what the far right largely do. That is why militarism forms such a strong emotional system for the far right: it contains the necessary vitality, order and adjacency to death, as well as, crucially, a certain degree of mindlessness, of giving up thought. Militarism is woven into the fascist imaginary. The opposite of total masculine failure is the fantasy of the martial life.

One common meme depicts a 'before-and-after' to this transition. Before: an overweight fedora-wearing man with

Richard Dawkins and Sargon of Akkad posters and a KEK flag[8] on the wall, living in a city in a filthy room. After: a clean-cut man seated at a desk with fields visible through the window, an AR-15 assault rifle, an Algiz rune flag on the wall and a Generation Identity sticker on their computer monitor.[9] The transition here is not from normie to hero: it is from alt-right internet-debater to heavily-armed rural ecofascist.

Civic nationalists often idealise the military as a foundational aspect of society. Many of their core concerns revolve around the betrayal of serving soldiers or veterans by the state and the left. The UK civic nationalist wave that took up much of the 2010s – the English Defence League, Tommy Robinson, and the DFLA[10] – started with outrage against a small Islamist protest of a procession of soldiers returning from Iraq. The pan-European Generation Identity organised training camps where recruits were drilled in martial arts. The US paramilitary group The Base boasted of the military and intelligence connections of its personnel – talk on its Discord server (a private web forum) was densely woven with military acronyms and phrases.[11]

However, for fascists, the state that controls the military is degenerate. And militarism is distinct from the military. Western armies are today distant from political power, and moreover strive to merely technologically dominate their enemies. As opposed to the experience of the First World War operationalised by the Nazis, the image of the military today is hi-tech and unerringly precise in action and thought – a far cry from more direct forms of masculine potency.

Indeed, Ernst Jünger, whose celebration of military life substantially influenced the fantasies of classical fascism, decried the distance and technological complexity of modern war as undermining personal heroism. Militarism nevertheless expresses the violent 'truth' of the world liberalism has sought to obscure: everything competes for domination.

Although atomised, the fascist subject has its crowd – or its pack, its swarm – often organised (at least rhetorically) around militaristic values. It is fealty to this community that comes to define fascists' lives. Radicalisation into the group is a process of immense emotional depth, and, for many, escaping from the far right is complicated most of all by having to give up these emotional attachments. Joining such a group requires other ties (to friends, family, and colleagues) to be broken down.

These groups are not all alike: the smaller the group and the clearer its structure, the more it opposes itself to society. Whereas marchers on a DFLA demonstration can imagine themselves as the voice of a substantial demographic, now lost or submerged by political correctness, the medium-sized groups such as Generation Identity imagine themselves to be restoring a kind of naturalised masculine subjectivity that has been eroded by the left – they organise for the return of the potent man. Further to the right, among the blackpilled neo-Nazis, these groups are almost entirely defined against the norms of society and undergo quasi-rituals to enforce this separation. From the declarative anti-semitism of National Action to the intragroup murders of Atomwaffen, the principle of these acts is 'we are absolutely different; we can never go back'.[12]

Misogyny is as various on the far-right as it is in wider society, but more glaring. Incels – a tributary of the far right, but not identical to them – are interested not so much in women as in control of women, or access to them. Feminism's successes in giving women control over themselves have frustrated this particular form of masculine desire. These notions of access and possession are crucial. Elliot Rodgers, spree killer and incel hero, articulates his right to access women in terms of his possession of luxury goods.[13] His wish for the markers of bourgeois normality is transformed into murderous rage. Where incels like Rodgers differ from fascists is in their admission that they are not at the top of the hierarchy. The 'virgin/chad' and 'alpha/beta' binaries allow different sections of the internet far right to place themselves according to their politics. Hopeless incels cast themselves squarely as virgin betas, and express their condition through pathetic acts of self-flagellation – and sometimes by carrying out acts of mass violence. For both incels and fascists, access to women embodies this hierarchy. And for both, the distinction between the top and the bottom is an essentially biological one. Sexuality, then, is a hierarchy, and a hierarchy whose spoils are apportioned by nature.

These strands come together in the work of F. Roger Devlin. His essay, 'Sexual Utopia in Power', published in a white nationalist journal, opens with "the collapse of white birth rates", and details the disadvantageous sexual situation of white Western men, both individually and as a group. Feminism, he says, has made women 'hypergamous' (although, inconsistently, he also suggests they always were). They seek to 'marry-up'. For Devlin, hypergamy may be bad for men – their sexual needs are unfairly not met – but for the white race as a whole it is catastrophic. If there aren't enough white children, the race will die. Like this, sexual anxiety becomes racial politics. Importantly, it's not a question of adding on racism later. The far-right is suffused with racial thinking, either explicitly or at a slight remove through hierarchies of religions or cultures. Idealised fascist masculinity is always white masculinity. For some fascists, white masculinity is the masculinity of imperial, globe-conquering, women-protecting, natural violence.

A man who cannot 'acquire' and control women – *and in doing so, keep them at bay* – is a 'cuck'. It names men as weak – it insinuates they cannot 'control their woman', or prevent them from having sex with other men, often black. This pithy term manages to synthesise all the psychosexual components of the far right: racialised sexual anxiety, in which black men in particular are seen as threateningly potent; a possessive and aggressive attitude towards women, in which women are 'acquired' much like any other possession; and a disgust at non-normative sexual relationships. Women who fall outside the capacity for neat acquisition are hated, or thought disgusting. Transwomen in particular are singled out for disgust: they are considered on the far right to be both men who have failed at being men and as 'fake' women. Unacquireable, unacquiring, trans and non-binary people unsettle the sexual heirarchy and patriarchal family unit.

Cuck is one slur in a bestiary of terms generated in the maelstrom of far-right internet discourse. The figures of the 'simp' or the 'white knight' are similar to the 'cuck' in their depiction of inferior or otherwise subservient men prostrating themselves for the attention, sexual or otherwise, of women. These categories must be frenetically reproduced to maintain their purchase. Browse any popular incel forum and you will see threads devoted to the confirmation of the original poster's self-hatred, pictures of anodyne faces forensically critiqued for flaws, a sense of raw abjectness that can only be sustained through active participation in mutual psychological harm. In this very abjectness, terms like 'cuck', 'simp' and 'beta' act as internal group discipline, keeping participants away from healthy support structures and trapped further in the morass. The pack is a site, mostly, of a collective bullying that stands in for solidarity. Keep your friends by keeping them at arm's length.

Some on the far right diagnose a 'devirilisation' of men, a symptom of a wider malaise in the West. Like this, sexual relationships become the model for all relationships, which must be relations of domination or they are nothing.

Theweleit identifies in the Freikorps a disgust with the 'swamp' of women and the 'flood' of communism. All around them, degeneracy. But degeneracy can encompass many things; in fact, its conceptual nebulousness is what allows the fascist to find evidence of it everywhere. However, it is often keenly focused: on queer sexual relationships most publicly, but also other behaviours that fall outside of traditional fascist conceptions of the family, such as casual or pre-marital sex (or even condoms), drug-taking or, as we will explore here, pornography.

How does the far right respond to pornography? It goes without saying that they partake. But what of their explicit political responses? Mark Collett – leader of the far-right Patriotic Alternative – has called it "anti-white hatred".[14] The 'entrance exam' for the neo-Nazi forum 'Fascist Forge' asked for the prospective member's views on 'Jews, homosexuals, pornography'.[15] Porn is degenerate, they say. It cucks men, distracts them from the production of white children, and besides, they say, it's run by the Jews. Pornography has become incorporated into a wider conspiracy, one prong of the attack on Western civilisation and the white race.

Whatever your impression of mainstream pornography, it is undeniable that it shows bodies as distinctly unequal. It makes worthy of attention certain bodies and hides others, although the sorting of these bodies is not as obvious nor as hegemonic as it was in pornography of the 60s and 70s – a process that fascists read as a decline in beauty standards. It shows racialised bodies indexed exclusively to their genitals:

the glee with which scenes from the interracial porn site BLACKED are posted to fascist internet forums by other fascists seeking to rile them up shows how potent these images are.

Porn, then, far from being an unambiguous expression of superiority for the white male viewer, cuts in all directions. The hierarchies and conspiracies encapsulated in pornography are reflective of wider fascist narratives: the Jews who control the porn industry (who you think are smarter than you but, you comfort yourself, sexually inadequate) persuade you, through enticements you are understandably unable to resist, to watch Black men (who you think are more sexually potent than you but, you comfort yourself, stupid) having sex with white women (who find you disgusting but who, you comfort yourself, are an essentially fallen group). In this way, one crucial psychological story – that you are simultaneously more and less powerful than your enemies, whose power *comes directly from their deficiency* – can be articulated in three different ways: against Jews, Black people, and women.

The theorist Andrea Long Chu has claimed that the consumption of pornography is a mode of feminisation – a way of making the spectator into a *thing* whose desires are produced for them by pornography.[16] It is perhaps *being turned into a thing* – a transformation which undermines the illusion of their sovereign, masculine, individuality – to which the far right's anti-pornography stance responds. This rejection of pornography might also articulate a more general truth: that consumption, particularly compulsive consumption, strips people of their selfhood. That porn comes through the highly mediated apparatus of the internet, as the most immediate and perfect commodity, even, as the all-consuming condition of our age, the nymph in the swamp of Jewish consumption, lends the rejection of pornography the character of a personal quest against the modern world.

Fascists portray their enemies' enjoyment of the commoditised world as effeminacy; their hatred is channelled into the open-mouthed elation of the soyboy. The fascist understands himself to be pushing against this form of stupefaction and the soyboy's excessive, grey, undifferentiated happiness in commoditised triviality. The 'coomer' (a variant on the generational 'boomer' and 'zoomer' archetypes) is someone who has let themselves go, given themselves over to pleasure, lost all ability to think for themselves or to make distinctions amidst the onslaught of dopaminergic commodities. In seeking out only what gives them narcissistic pleasure, the soyboy and the coomer grey themselves out into the background of the world. This greyed-out enemy is the contemporary figure of 'the last man'.

This talk of fascist resistance to trivialising commodities suggests a relationship to class; however, far-right actors aren't obviously motivated by class interest. Why? First, far-right politics are complex, even chaotic. Ideologies are strange, syncretic, and muddied. For the most part, opportunism reigns. It is perhaps important to stress again and again the non-ideological character of much contemporary radicalisation. When there is an explicit ideology in play, it is fixated predominantly on culture or on race, the latter an intensification of the former.

Nor is it possible, we think, to read fascist movements as clearly representing the interests of one particular social or economic class. At a push, the interests of the far right might be aligned with a particular fraction of the bourgeoisie, as was the case with some of the far-right populist politics of the last 5 years. More generally, the ecology of far-right movements is sufficiently diverse to take in all classes: upper-class racists go to their eugenics meetings, publish under pseudonyms, and fund groups and individuals; the petite bourgeoisie flock to the large street movements or become social media grifters; the posh young professionals try and muck in and scarper at the first sign their career is on the line; the socially rejected go to UK Yellow Vest demos.[17]

Fascist communities don't share a single class relationship to capitalism, but they do largely have a consumption-focused relationship to society. The petite bourgeoisie understand their problem as essentially one of attempting to drum up sufficient consumption, aristocrats are essentially consumptive, and the disaffected young men populating NEET spaces online lack any relationship to society except through consumption. This relation of consumption lets one read society as degraded: the petit-bourgeoisie become frustrated that consumers seem interested only in the mass-produced commodities from the larger capitalists;

the aristocrats can despair at the decline of popular tastes; and NEETs hate the commodities they consume and are consumed by, particularly porn. In each case, the uncertainty about one's place in society, and perhaps the feeling that one is something of a consumptive parasite, leads to a psychological need to disavow capitalism itself and decry its degrading tendencies, while simultaneously affirming all its governing separations such as race, gender, and to some extent class.

In the 'jobless recovery' from the Great Financial Crisis, to some on the far right it seemed that all the new value was accruing to jobs defined by the gendered 'soft skills' or sex – exemplified by the OnlyFans model. The far-right distortion, so productive of rage, runs that as men were pushed to working in Amazon warehouses, women used their biological advantage to make vastly more money lounging around taking nudes for simps on the internet, gaining status in the process. In truth, as with most economic crises, women suffered more. Despite the attempts by some to frame the far right as the 'true' workers' movement, solidarity amongst workers is impossible if both women and people of colour are thought to be imposters in the category.

Finding themselves unattractive, and being found unattractive in their turn; finding themselves unemployed and being, indeed, unemployable, truly surplus to the world: these consumers without production and without the cognitive or organisational tools to make work a site of struggle, turn towards consumption and circulation as the site of struggle, because that is what it genuinely is for them. As Theodor W. Adorno and Max Horkheimer say, the idea that "the circulation sphere is responsible for exploitation is a socially necessary illusion."[18] Now, when the quintessential commodity has become an OnlyFans subscription, this feeling of being a permanent consumer without a grip on the world subsumes young men on their way to fascism in this illusion. Attempts to fight this struggle can easily become a rejection of the world of commodities, and an assertion of a masculine refusal to be seduced. Couple this need to escape the 'slimy bourgeois mire' with anti-semitic conspiracy theories about Jewish control of pornography – the most psychologically complicated and intense form of consumption – and this escalates into a central issue of control and power in the fascist imaginary.

The feelings of fascists, then, are intimately linked to failure, masculinity, the military, group-belonging, virility, consumption and its attendant narrative of degeneracy, anti-semitic conspiracies, racial hierarchies, sexual anxiety, the lost imperial history of Europe, misogyny, a simultaneous assertion of helplessness and power, the structural conditions of life under capitalism, and the 'acquisition' of women.

Once stimulated, these emotions, (inadequacy, hate, alienation) must be made to march. They must not just march in the heads of those who feel them but also persuade others to join in, providing validation for these feelings that won't fade. Mostly far from power, the far right does so through a process of propagandising and manipulation organised around a strategy, or the semblance of a strategy, known as 'metapolitics'.

METAPOLITICS
AND AESTHETICS

———

L ong before Twitter, 8chan and the alt right, the far right was online. Like many marginal ideologies and subcultures, far-right and fascist activists were early adopters of new means of communication, and recognised the potential the internet had for circumventing media gatekeepers. As far back as 1985, the Anti-Defamation League (ADL) released the 'Computerized Networks of Hate' report,[19] detailing the emergence of the 'Aryan Nation Liberty Net' and the innocuous-sounding 'Info International'. Most such early efforts were reflections of existing IRL networks. Similarly, Stormfront was founded to support David Duke's 1990 campaign for US Senate, before being re-established in 1996 as a forum for white nationalists to communicate and socialise[20] (although its autonomy from existing networks remained limited, and so too did its visibility).

However, with the increasing permeability of platforms, the viral logic of outrage and offence spread from the ungoverned spaces of the internet through Reddit, Facebook and YouTube, and then into Telegram channels, Discord servers and new alternative 'free speech' platforms, and the far right's visibility began to increase. Suddenly, around 2015, they seemed to be everywhere online. The internet's most spectacular political movements were no longer the global anti-authoritarian struggles of 2010-2014 but the alt-right. These networks were almost entirely separated from existing IRL organising. Indeed, when they did crash back into the physical world, such as at the Charlottesville rally of 2017, groups formed online – in a mirror image of the earlier failures of far-right groups to move *onto* the internet – rapidly found themselves out of their depth and at odds with each other.[21]

THE QUESTION OF 'METAPOLITICS'

The far right sometimes thinks of their disparate online activities (posting memes, organising Facebook groups, running magazines, recording podcasts, making anti-semitic Florence and the Machine remix videos) as 'metapolitics' – a term that names the strategy of influencing culture so as to influence politics. The idea has one of its earliest theorists in Antonio Gramsci, but the version operative on the far right now is simpler: "politics is downstream of culture". According to Daniel Friberg (a far-right identitarian organiser and publisher from Sweden), "Metapolitics is a war of social transformation, at the level of worldview, thought, and culture."[22] Far-right groups such as Generation Identity have seen their purpose explicitly in such terms, as have many far-right influencers, swarm-members, and some intellectuals.

Theories of metapolitics on the far-right originated in the European New Right (ENR or *Nouvelle Droite*), a far-right intellectual movement that stood in opposition to both the left-wing uprisings of 1968 and a mainstream right it saw as capitulating to American influence. The ENR was hostile to equality, multiculturalism and liberal democracy, and proposed instead a form of differentialist racism (in which no race is supreme, but all are radically incompatible), a form of racism still called upon by far-right actors today who wish to downplay their own extremity. Their politics, a kind of revolutionary conservatism they hoped would instigate a new era for a rejuvenated white European culture, were couched in a complex pseudo-philosophical language they thought would produce a new far-right intellectual culture.

There is not one unified approach to metapolitics. Far from it. Impatience with the glacial pace of cultural change the strategy implies led to schisms within the ENR as early as the 1970s. Since then, this same move – in which a more impatient faction abandons the 'metapolitical' strategy for more radical and faster action – has been repeated across the far right – for example, by the writer Guillaume Faye. Faye's supposedly faster-paced metapolitics is itself distinct from the more nebulous metapolitics of the wider far right, where it operates not as an explicit strategy but as a collection of opportunist campaigns. Faye's *Why We Fight* may be a seminal text of modern metapolitics, but it is hard to imagine Tommy Robinson religiously returning to its hugely bloated glossary to check on the definition of 'ethnopluralism'.[23] Nevertheless, much of Robinson's activity clearly is comprehensible within the framework of 'metapolitics': it seems one doesn't even have to know one is doing it. One might even end up doing 'metapolitics' despite rejecting it. Mark Collett of the far-right group Patriotic Alternative has criticised metapolitics and has affirmed instead conventional political organising.[24] He nevertheless engages principally in the same kind of cultural work that 'metapolitics' seeks to name. If metapolitics contains all these things, what does it *not* contain?

We can juxtapose 'metapolitics' to its opposite: electoral politics. In 2016, white nationalist Richard Spencer said, "I don't think elections are the way you change the world. You change the world through major cultural changes."[25] And Friberg in 2015: "Any parliamentary struggle must be preceded, legitimised, and supported by a metapolitical struggle. Metapolitics, at its best, reduces parliamentarism to a question of mere formalities."[26] And yet, even in this apparently straightforward juxtaposition there is uncertainty. Perhaps the most famous example of far-right 'metapolitics' – the 'meme magic' of the alt-right in 2016 – was precisely an attempt to win an election. What are we to make of this apparent inclusion of elections as the object of metapolitics? Perhaps this 'strategy' is not so opposed to electioneering.

What about another political tactic: mass shootings? Surely, they are not 'metapolitics'? Deadly violence might seem, indeed, to be the exact opposite of slow-moving metapolitical transformation. The Pittsburgh synagogue shooter posted "Screw your optics, I'm going in" on Gab before killing 11 people. As disillusionment with Trump has grown, *strictly* extra-electoral politics has returned, but now focused on a more radical creed that opposes both political solutions and the 'metapolitical' strategy entirely. Yet metapolitics and deadly violence are still engaged in a relationship, in which the 'radicalism' of the murderers is counterposed with the 'moderateness' of the more image-inclined far right. Thus, in the wake of the Christchurch mosque shootings, where 51 people were murdered, Generation Identity UK was interviewed on the BBC's flagship current affairs program Newsnight to explain their 'Great Replacement' theory – the name of the shooter's manifesto. This is not to say that either the mass murderers or the metapoliticians are acting deliberately: this is one of many cases in which the dynamics of movements exceed their actors' intentions.

Might 'metapolitics', then, not name the overarching strategy of the far right, but instead be just an occasionally reached-for term to thread disparate activity retrospectively into the appearance of a strategy?

It's true that people on the far right engage in 'metapolitics'; it's not true that activity on the far right is organised around a singular strategy called 'metapolitics'. The distinction matters: first, it dispels the illusion of coherence and strategic clarity and enables us to see the conflicting, improvised and inept quality of much far-right activity. And second, it allows us to think more clearly about the relationship between the far right and the internet. Metapolitics is a politics in which attempts to change culture and spread information predominate. We might ask, then: is this supposedly cohesive strategy of the post-internet far right emerging simply because it 'runs along the grooves' of the internet? That is, does this supposed strategy not require the far right to conceptualise it consistently because 'metapolitics' is simply how the internet makes its participants act *by default?* The internet has a well-known logic of virality that always had a political character. Kony 2012 was perhaps the first moment on the internet where a practice of awareness-raising – the idea that distributing information *was itself already a politics* – crystallised. And if this is just one pronounced moment in a history of *politics transforming itself wholesale into metapolitics* – if the struggle for cultural transformation simply *is* the game of the internet – what connection might this have to the desire for control contained within far-right politics and fascism itself?

CULTURE AND FASCISM

Culture did not become a concern for fascism through the ENR. Classical fascism conceived of the state as 'absolute', and its absoluteness contained all aspects of culture. This required the saturation of life by fascism and the total command of information. This totalising character – the transformation of all private space into public space, and all private activity into a component or antagonist of the fascist cause – was possible only with the arrival, in the 20th century, of mass communication technologies like the radio (the *Volksempfänger*). Albert Speer, speaking at the Nuremberg Trials, said, "Through technical devices like the radio and loudspeaker, 80 million people were deprived of independent thought."[27] Nazism strove towards including within itself all the cultural activities of the population – at its limit, their every thought and waking moment – as an object for political control. Cultural transformation, then, is integral to fascist politics, and even its bureaucratic actions are cultural in the widest sense – statecraft becomes 'metapolitics'.

The far right on the internet today is of course nothing like the *Volksempfänger*. 'Culture' as the unifying spirit of a mythic *volk* has slipped to 'culture' as a Bitchute[28] channel with 100 subscribers. But that doesn't mean we should rule out the possibility of the latter producing, at scale, the former. And scale they do. Individual pieces of far-right content often have very little to say for themselves, but the constant churn of content – livestreams, blogs, podcasts – has an effect; quantity has its own quality. Fascist parties were often quasi-total institutions[29] – their participants were able to live their entire lives through them, even against the opposition of the majority. Now, that totality is provided by the streamification of ideas and the endless content feed. The sense of a gradually arriving apocalyptic showdown can be conjured out of trivialities because the news consumer is always doomscrolling to the next thing. Reflection is never required; instead, a sense of dread mounts. The flow between videos, podcasts, threads – pieces of apparently isolated content – is up to you, and highly individualised, but all depict a world of detailed yet nebulous threats.

On the wider internet as on the far right, the personal cycles into the public and back again with increasing tempo and at ever-more granular levels – different comments, different adverts, different posts are served to you and your closest friends in what has nevertheless come to *feel* like public space. If classical fascism strove to subsume the private into the public, the question of how the far right relates to the internet's deformation of public space today is an intricate and important one.

Life before the internet was more separated out into distinct personal and public domains; now, people's politics are publicly visible by default. At the same time, perhaps, there is no longer one coherent thing called 'the public' on which influence can work. The culture of the far right online often notes this fractured society – a move sometimes radicalising (because this unified public must therefore be *forcibly made*) or sometimes driving towards various forms of separatism (because this unified public is irrecoverable). Although control over other people's private lives is often sought through the reactionary cultural politics of the far right, they have consistently resisted attempts to control their own spaces online, and their activities have fractured the internet (and therefore the public) still further. As the internet moved from scattered, broadly anonymous communities in the 1990s to communities defined almost entirely by the mirroring online of offline existence, the relationship between anonymity and trust modulated across digital space as it did across society more generally.

The internet that had, in its earlier years, catered for those who felt themselves powerless IRL, changed with the arrival of Facebook and other 'normie' forms of real-name social media. The alt-right began in the secretive 'masked' culture of imageboards and came to despise this normalisation. A central theme of the ENR – the (chiefly American) push for global cultural homogeneity and hegemony – became the 'globohomo' conspiracy. The term names the bland homogenous international liberalism promoted by corporations whose quintessential moment is perhaps the corporate sponsorship of Pride events (in examples such as this, the far right contends, the left is simply the dupe of capital). Against this flattening masquerading as diversity, the alt-right posed a culture of ribaldry, aggression, and extremism.

On this fractured internet, the far right radicalises, not because the internet is ungoverned, but because it is governed inconsistently.[30] Much as in epidemiology, it is neither the city nor the peri-urban spaces adjacent to it that drive the emergence of zoonotic viruses, but the disjointed and uneven circulation of capital, goods, and regulation between the two.

Smaller groups can spiral towards greater and greater radicalism in private space before returning to operations on the wider web. 'Raids' are organised against enemy ('normie') websites or games, often organised from other platforms, in which shocking images, political slogans or trolling are used to disrupt and propagandise. Raids can border on the banal – a mass disliking of a YouTube video, for example – but their true power comes with the illicit thrill of invading another space: logging onto child-friendly online game Habbo Hotel, saying the n-word and forming swastikas with your characters, for example. More recently, the tactic of 'Groyping' has emerged, which will address in Chapter 4, The Swarm and the Influencer. The very ubiquity and speed of the net – that things are happening constantly and, increasingly, content is going out live – makes these raids almost impossible to prevent entirely.

However, there is nowhere entirely out of the reach of governance. Even so-called 'wild west media' like the dark web are monitored and subject to interventions from state authorities. This is not necessarily through censure. Sometimes misinformation and disruption are used instead.[31] True believers, or covert operatives pretending to be such, almost always seem to find a deeper corner of the internet to gather and exchange information. There, the tools of the state become less and less transparently effective, but the possibility of intervention remains a source of constant anxiety – pushing groups deeper underground. When applied recursively, this cycle of governance, paranoia, and clandestinity produces the 'extremification process' we will discuss later.

In the rest of this chapter, we will outline more of the emerging trends, tactics, and dynamics of far-right politics online.

EMERGENT TACTICS

Ironic detachment

Sometimes, saying something masks a belief in its opposite. On the internet, the ability to disavow or detach yourself from your own actions is famously pronounced. This has become such a general condition of being online that it matters little what the intention actually is. Densely occupied online space produces flourishing communities around the organising topic, regardless of whether the posters take themselves to be serious or not. Some of the components of the far-right online ecology, such as the subreddit The_Donald, were created ironically but quickly mutated into spaces for sincere supporters. On the other side of this, liberal audiences have been trained through years of looking at 'critical art' to read the appearance of even the most brazenly affirmatory of gestures as 'critique'. Such a reading habit numbed inquisitive browsers to the starkness of the politics of the alt-right in their early days and facilitated the affectation of a faux-outraged stance by journalists who interviewed them.

Memes

The alt-right's 'meme war' framing of the 2015-16 US presidential campaign is not entirely absurd. Successful memes work because they delineate real, very general, patterns in the world. They participate in a playful dynamic of abstraction and absurdity. Their spread relies on fitting highly various situations into the same basic pattern. To make the patterns you think in spread is a precondition to making your worldview the default one.

The cast of characters in memes, despite the situations in which they find themselves being numerous, are quite limited. Indeed, the organisation of the world into a cast of stock characters is a precondition for much far-right politics (although it's obviously not sufficient). The image of a world oriented around the typical, and completely inevitable, behaviour of 'chads', 'betas', 'femoids' (a derogatory term for women), and so on, rather than around the nuanced behaviour of real people, can be itself radicalising. If people are destined to simply perform the actions of their 'type', the world as a whole can only be replaced entirely, or completely destroyed. We can think about these images in terms of an alternating invocation of 'primitive and brink,'[32] aesthetic forms in keeping with the tension between radicalism and conventionality across the far right. On the one hand, primality and transhistorical truth (the absoluteness of race, the behaviour of all women, etc.); on the other, the most radically new and extreme themes (extreme violence, futuristic technologies, the bleeding edge of the world).

This 'meme war' framing is still with us today in the embers of the alt-right, glowing from Telegram chats. There, they make 'fashwave' images, mimicking vaporwave images with Nazi imagery as source material. The alt-right was experienced by its participants as a moment of a sudden spectacular disruption in the distribution of worldly power. In its long and still writhing tail, the symbols it used can seem like they themselves possessed the power that drove this disruption. The network effects, or the social novelty of the movement, or the situation of widespread social crisis can be forgotten. This fetishisation of the tactics of the 'meme war' themselves – 'just show them the potent symbol of the swastika and they will be converted' – hardens around what we might call the far right's 'mytho-aesthetic' wing. The far right disconnects its tactics and its symbols from their novelty, their momentariness, and, ultimately, their social character. It is a mistake we should be at pains not to make as well.

The memes of Britain First – a far right group in the UK – were many and varied. In between bland 'Support our Troops' messages widely shared on their (now deleted) Facebook page, they posted Islamophobic and anti-migrant memes. The anodyne memes generated likes and follows, which allowed Islamophobic politics to be injected directly into followers' Facebook feeds. As increasingly stringent platform rules have been developed, this tactic of mixing hooks and inflammatory content has become harder to sustain.

Memes can also become stunts when they move into the real world. One of the most important stunts had a dumbfounding simplicity: a stickering campaign of bland stickers that stated in *sans serif*, "It's ok to be white". Memes, which circulate like viruses, pass from person to person in an endless chain of mutation. The "It's okay to be white" meme is like a virus that triggers a massive overreaction from the immune system. It is this which ultimately kills those infected.

Slang and codes

What is 'the Boogaloo' and why do its adherents wear Aloha shirts with their AR-15s? Why is everyone in this picture standing around in Fred Perry shirts making the scuba diving 'OK' sign? Why did the Christchurch shooter refer to himself as a 'kebab removalist'? Swarm harassment[33] works to partition the internet, and in the partitioned internet, argots develop. While some of this slang is meant to stand out (triple brackets (((like this))) are often used on the far right to signal the names of Jews – and by Jews and non-Jews alike to undermine the practice) other parts of it are meant to be almost completely innocuous. The 'black sun' symbol – a symbol made from 12 radial 'sig' runes – used by the SS is often used now in jurisdictions, such as Germany, where the swastika is banned. It is not widely known, and it allows communication between groups who do recognise it. The use of pagan iconography, such as the Odal (ᛟ) rune, performs a similar function, with the added aspect that it gives a plausible way around accusations of fascism, as the symbol has other connotations. Similarly, a style of talking has developed that attempts to conceal one's 'power level' (how racist one is). The Patriotic Weekly Review YouTube show by Mark Collett, for example, trades in highly-deniable but obvious antisemitism (the Bitchute version of the same has no such subtleties).

Another tactic involves taking common symbols – the OK sign and particular popular brands – and absorbing them as symbols of the far right. Such tactics put the far right's enemies on edge, and make their size impossible to accurately determine. There are still more subtle versions of this same process, for example hijacking the once innocuous 'feels guy' meme or, indeed, Pepe the Frog. In new versions of the wojak memes, stock characters (which were once differentiated on their choice of beverage) are differentiated on the basis of their optimism about forming an ethnostate.

Stunts

The above tactics largely play out online. The far right does act IRL, but into a physical world that incorporates the digital. Stunts aim to shock, entertain and outrage, and most of all capture attention. Unlike direct action, it is not necessary for stunts to have any material impact on the world, although they sometimes do. They fulfil the demands of the cult of action. They are, performatively, the opposite of conspiracies: they say, "here, at last, something without dissimulation, something *out in the open*."

The 1934 Nazi Party Congress, filmed by Leni Riefenstahl for her propaganda film *Triumph of the Will*, was planned with the camerawork in mind. Similarly, far-right stunts today are performed *in order* to be seen online. Whereas for Riefenstahl the distribution of the film was assured by the Nazi Party itself, now the dissemination of a stunt depends on the virality of its content, so the message must be calibrated not only to say the right thing to its eventual audience, but also to be taken on its way by those who share it out of outrage. This economy of distribution means that the classical fascist spectacle of order, while still a far-right fixation, is secondary now to the spectacles of action and crass offensiveness.

Images of spectacular disorder are popular regardless of political origin. Riots are direct action. Without mediation, people take what they need. Nevertheless, they are also highly mediatised events, continually drawn into the growing flow of images of disorder. Far-right groups with a law-and-order slant, such as some elements of the Boogaloo Bois and the American militia movement, respond to these images of looting with their own spectacle of order, but it is only when that order shows itself for the chaotic violence it is, such as in the case of Kyle Rittenhouse, that they gain traction as a spectacular image.

As ever, the action that most far-right stunts evoke is both violent and banal. Generation Identity endangers migrants' lives in the Mediterranean to call for EU countries to implement their own border laws. The DFLA calls for even heavier policing of Muslim communities. The masculine subject represented by these actions counterposes themselves to a state that has supposedly shrunk from its masculine duties, or become soft. This is obviously nonsense: deportations in the UK are at an all-time high, whilst the PREVENT programme is used extensively to oppress communities of colour. The callous brutality of European states is conspicuous in its response to mass deaths in the Mediterranean. The far right here is merely the leading edge of the *status quo*. Indeed, three members of GI were found guilty of "exercising activities in conditions that could create confusion with a public function" for their stunt in an Alpine pass – essentially impersonating the state. Despite their cult of action and vitality, they exist to express the most explicit part of the governance of Western societies, not against it.

The stunts of GI or the mosque invasions of Britain First are not just spectacle. GI's Defend Europa boat was echoed by paramilitary Greek fascists shooting at refugees in the Aegean Sea, and Britain First's mosque invasions by acts of terroristic violence in London's mosques. These stunts do not merely act as propagandistic spectacle but are rehearsals, or templates, for actions in which real violence is enacted.[34]

The next three chapters are on forms of metapolitics: conspiracy theories, the digital swarm and social media influencers (taken together), and the right's intellectuals. Each of these parts of the far right builds on the last towards greater and greater degrees of articulation of a political worldview. We have separated them out for clarity, but we should keep in mind that these processes of articulation do not act independently of each other. Instead, they act on each other, both in a supportive capacity and antagonistically. We will show how these various forms of support and antagonism construct the dynamic ecosystem of the post-internet far right.

DEEP STATE

CONSPIRACY THEORY

Flat Earthers, Anti-vaxxers, Coronavirus, Jeffrey Epstein: the period since 9/11 has brought a discordant parade of conspiracies to the mainstream. In our socially stressed and narrativistically uncertain times, official accounts start to seem brittle and uncertain, always one conspiratorial gotcha away from total collapse. There are no commonly circulating explanations for how the world works, no systems of thought to rely on.

This might seem to make metapolitics (of whatever type) more difficult: conspiracies, like viruses, spread without centralised coordination, and prevent any one group from directing the flows of explanation entirely. The far right's conspiratorial narratives are just as susceptible to being undercut as any other explanation. But the general condition does benefit them: rising uncertainty is fertile ground for far-right conspiracy, where moral simplicity, a baroque intricacy masquerading as sophistication, and operationalised prejudice thrive. Although informational chaos doesn't spread *only* the ideas of the far right, it benefits them more than anyone else.

Conspiracy theories are the recruiting tools of the far right, but they are also its paradigmatic mode of thought. We might even ask if there is anything to distinguish far-right conspiracies from others. Might, as Andrew Wilson has suggested, the "extent of far-right usage of conspiracy theory [mean] that an articulation of current conspiracy theories is to evoke political positions on the extreme right, wittingly or not?"[35]

The psychological explanation for conspiracies is obvious: the world, which is an intimidating and increasingly confusing place to be in, can be made simple. All its complexities – and the intense sense of ignorance that one must face when trying to say anything – can be reduced into a single narrative. Better yet, this narrative is flattering to an individual's prior beliefs about themselves, others, or the groups to which they belong. Conspiracy theories' explanatory simplicity, which cuts cleanly through thick jungles of information, comes at the price of any tests for truth. Because explanations go untested, they feel deeply true, even certain, as they fit flush to your most basic prior beliefs. This can feel like 'thinking for yourself' – maintaining a certain intellectual hygiene – which is rare and pleasant in our informational deluge. As society demands more and more cognitive power to navigate, explanatory ability becomes a defining marker of a person's worth, and turns explanation into a saleable commodity hawked by far-right influencers.

Why, despite this apparent freedom to think anything, do the contents of conspiracy theories follow such predictable patterns? It's not mere individual psychology that explains the often-predictable themes of conspiracies – their texture and uptake is afforded by the organisation of society. Our prior beliefs are not simply stuck in our heads, rather, they circulate, are played out in practice, and are selected at a wider social level.

There is no exhaustive list of where this selection might happen. After neoliberalism shredded the sites of democratic contestation, conspiracy theories provided a site for antagonism to be expressed. The traditional sense-making institutions of society are present here mostly negatively, as everything that conspiracists resist, although arguably news organisations in the Anglophone world have taken a turn for the conspiratorial too – perhaps most prominently The Sun's publishing of neo-Nazi conspiracy theory materials in 2019.[36] Instead, we must look to an ever-expanding list of dark and private places to see where this bubbling of conspiratorial thinking is going on: in conversations and their disappointments, in political organising and its failures, in individual hunts for information online, in the slow drifting apart of already atomised individuals, in a rapidly swelling and ramifying sense of personal betrayal.

Broad social and technical changes have shifted the landscapes in which conspiracy communities form. They are obviously not exclusively modern phenomena – anti-semitic conspiracies, for example, have been operative for far longer. But their density has increased in the modern period, and accelerated further since the rise of the internet.

Why? Sociologist Luc Boltanski argues that, in modernity, national boundaries of predictable reality have been overrun by capitalism's international drive. As capitalism overflows these stable sense-making boundaries, '*the reality of reality*' becomes suspicious – things start to seem uncertain at a profound level.[37]

Because there exist now, either on the far right or in society at large, almost no structured programme of political education, ideas can rarely be overturned wholesale – they must be changed piece by piece. It is this transformation that memes afford, in part. They shift from very amorphous perceptions of isolated phenomena to very high-level and general explanations.

In modernity, everything can seem to be coming from the outside: zoonotic viruses, hijacked airplanes, government intervention into life, alien masters of the universe. Conspiracy theories are often concerned intimately with space – not only with the location of the conspiracy's enormous distance from the conspiracist, but also with the need to localise power in space. In truth, of course, power *is* highly dispersed, nigh on unlocalisable. Fiat money, for example, is suspicious because it seems to be the mere assertion of the government's emanating power over society. It is juxtaposed often to the apparently clear, intrinsic, and localisable value of gold. Conspiracy theorists resist the distributed and complex character of modern life by reducing all manner of social stress to the *merely elaborate* effects of some more simple but overwhelming power. In the contemporary period, society's general mediatedness, violent complexity, and crisis-riddled quality, as well as pronounced uptick in volatility to life, make fertile terrain for conspiratorial thought.

Conspiracies have a complex relationship with detail. They focus on particular moments, often circulating around stunning but unexplained coincidence (more common the more complex the world becomes). However, they evaporate on specifics: they condense the 'gears level' account of how the world operates into increasingly general statements, become unconcerned by the mechanisms through which power operates, as well as increasingly (as they totalise) concerned only with a general clash of abstractions. They therefore become immensely intricate as they run up against their own inconsistency – an inconsistency that can be used as further proof of secrecy.

This inconsistency also lets them split apart and mutate into variations that differ depending on their hosts' proclivities. These variations are not necessarily antagonistic, and endless variation allows their spread. The image of conspiracy theorists as isolated is largely untrue; they form large and complex communities online and in person, communities with particular features that work to sustain the conspiracy's power. Indeed, community is a consequence of the conspiracy's strangeness, a strangeness that makes them spread like pathogens. The anxiety they bring must be externalised: release from the panic of seeing beneath the surface comes from retelling, momentarily easing disquiet at the cost of putting more of the conspiracy in the environment. Other people catch it, and they have the same reaction. Even at a low dose, it can be effective. Even if not explicitly believed, the conspiracy can morph your worldview, as one moment of doubt metastasises into another.

Online informational fragmentation is complex. This holographic stack of content, everything on top of each other, with the relations between them continually changing, lets people sift out information freely. This mixture of fragmentation, opacity, and world-wide accessibility (within certain limits) allows conspiracy-flourishing, as well as viral inescapability. The media architecture of the internet seems to lend itself to something like conspiracy: we are presented online not with a narrative thread to follow (unless we visit exclusively a single website or read a single blog, which is obviously atypical) but essentially a large and ever-expanding relational database, whose linkages are many but obscure, lending the force of finding connections itself a greater significance, even though their possible number is inconceivably vast.[38]

On some platforms, communities engage with events and arrange their ideas collectively, mechanisms that allow for a degree of coherence and stability to emerge, and for individuals to be held to account for their pasts, often in punitive ways. None of these conditions are true on imageboards. There, multiple users pick over events and content in a detailed way, without those explorations being in any way coordinated. The lack of stable identities means users can schism on their interpretations of things without the social group falling apart. Each to their own explanation. The most potent explanations escape the imageboard and make their way out into the wider more 'suburban' internet.

However, there is no straight arrow of conspiracy theories flowing from the darker internet to the lighter; they travel back and forth. What continual circulation drives is not necessarily greater political extremism, so much as amalgamation: QAnon, the ultimate (for now) conspiracy theory, whose subgroups take in everything from ancient aliens to chemtrails to baby-eating, is a product of this mash-up without limit.

QANON

In the era of Trump, how might conspiracy theorists become enamoured of state power? Having long been suspicious of the government, in all its forms, those on the far right who think of Trump as *their guy* must now work to resolve this contradiction. Enter QAnon. QAnon is a conspiracy theory which states that Donald Trump is fighting a complex and secret war against a paedophilic cabal in 'the deep state'. It is sustained online by a series of 'drops' – essentially, cryptic posts from the person also known as QAnon, who purports to be a high-ranking official in the US government, aware of this secret struggle. These posts on usually anonymous imageboards, each bearing the same cryptographic code, are picked over by a large group of conspiracists, all with their own particular interpretation of their exact meaning, but broadly in agreement on some major points.

This is somewhat anomalous among recent far-right conspiracy theories. Birtherism – the conspiracy that Barack Obama wasn't born in the US and was therefore ineligible to be President – was a piece of blatant racism and it fit a conventional logic. The Republican base needed to explain to itself its defeat. Similarly, the Jade Helm 15 theory stated that the government was preparing to put in place martial law under the cover of a military training exercise. A similar logic applies to conspiracies about the mass-shooting at Sandy Hook, where denying the reality of the violence shields oneself from the implication that gun violence is endemic to society.

In contrast, the first 'Q drop' came in October 2017 – *after* Donald Trump had won. Why would a victorious political force need a conspiracy? The election of Trump was experienced by many as an exhilarating disinhibition, a marker of almost total possibility. QAnon allows the far right to exist both as a government and as a movement, struggling *against* another, deeper, government. Conspiracy here resolves the contradiction between the movement-form and the state-form of far-right politics. In doing so it reveals that the disappointment to which QAnon attends is with Trump for not locking up the Clintons.

By reigniting this possibility, QAnon allows access to the distant figure of Trump. A felt personal connection with

Trump was enough for Anthony Comello, a Q follower, to murder Frank Cali – a New York crime boss who Comello believed was in the 'deep state' – under the impression that he was doing what Trump wanted. At the same time, QAnon allows for the conspiracy theorist far right to swing into line behind greater state control, operating under a fantasy in which the state is cleansed by a military operation involving both the military itself and the population at large. In its formation of a group who believe the truth has been revealed to them, QAnon – probably the most complexly syncretic movement in history – begins to resemble a religion.

In Germany, the *Reichsbürgerbewegung* (Reich Citizens' Movement), like 'sovereign citizens' and 'freemen on the land', believes that the modern German state is illegitimate. It has also been growing at a rapid pace, doubling since a member shot a police officer in 2016 to approximately 19,000 members.[39] Members of this conspiracy have syncretised it with QAnon. The international anti-lockdown demonstrations of 2020 were awash with QAnon's elaborate symbolic language.

This openness to other forms of thought – syncretism – has long been regarded as a fundamental component of fascist politics. The leaps and generalisations that syncretism implies are raised in QAnon to a high, directly weaponisable pitch: a form of political belief in which nothing is too grotesque to be believed about one's enemies. Child sex trafficking – the subject of many QAnon conspiracies – is simply the end result of a tendency towards debauchery that QAnon believers see in their demonic opponents. As it generalises further and targets more than just specific elites, it may come to serve very well as the cognitive foundations of a mass fascist movement.

WHITE EXTINCTION THEORY

On the far right, the theory of white extinction spawns endless variations. It has a simple core: white people are being slowly erased in a process of massive demographic transformation, either as the by-product of neoliberalism (or 'globalism') or through the deliberate actions of a particular group, most commonly Jews. This is, of course, false. Demographic change is highly abstract, but, as with the idea of degeneracy, 'evidence' is easy to come by – more or less any anecdotal experience with someone deemed insufficiently white can contribute to its confirmation. This abstractness – demographics is an almost technocratic concern – paradoxically lends the theory an apocalyptic air: proof is all around you, and thus it seems to warrant almost limitless violence.

Unlike QAnon, which is still distinctly subcultural (in form, if not necessarily size), white extinction theories permeate much of what the far right says, thinks and does. Forms can be found in far-right tendencies that share little in the way of strategy or presentation – from the prescriptions of race scientists to the manifestos of mass shooters. On the internet, white extinction theories, once the preserve of niche movements, can now command audiences of millions. The Christchurch shooter's manifesto, which contained such conspiracy theories, spread across the internet as his attack was streamed on Facebook.

Such theories are comprehensible only from a certain view of race: that racial identities are immutable and their boundaries strict; that those identities imply distinct and unchangeable cultural or genetic characteristics; and that 'civilisation' is a consequence of those characteristics. From this view spring two entailments: birth rates must be controlled (and ergo, some non-white people must be removed, be that through deportation or extermination); and white people must be induced to have children.

Conceptions of a white race under existential threat are not a product of the internet, nor are they in any way new. In 1920, eugenicist and Ku Klux Klan member Lothrop Stoddard published *The Rising Tide of Color Against White World-Supremacy* in which he bemoaned the decline of white birth rates, rising populations of non-white countries and the growing influence of nationalist movements in colonised countries which, he argued, would lead to the downfall of empire and the destruction of white supremacy.[40] It was largely a journalistic translation of Madison Grant's 1916 *The Passing of The Great Race*,[41] which was itself an updating and focusing of the works of European race theorists such as Arthur de Gobineau, Houston Stewart Chamberlain, and Georges Vacher de Lapouge. Richard Spencer wrote a forward for this latter book in 2013; Hitler called it his 'bible'. The theories expounded by these men bear a striking resemblance to the white extinction theories of today, although 'whiteness' in the earlier theories is more focused on its supposed 'Nordic' subtype. The boundaries of 'immutable racial types' turn out to be themselves somewhat changeable.

White extinction is a kind of synthesising theory, a property that makes it infinitely adaptable. It amalgamates race science, the misogynist need to control women's bodies, anti-semitism, assertions of insurmountable cultural difference, and, ultimately, apocalypticism. Certain aspects can be emphasised or de-emphasised to taste. The version taken up by identitarian movements in Europe, the 'Great Replacement', draws on Islamophobia to portray Muslims as 'occupiers',[42] controlled by nebulous 'replacist elites'. The White Genocide Manifesto, authored by neo-Nazi David Lane, is more explicit, naming a 'Zionist conspiracy' intent on exterminating the 'White race'.[43] The former has found greater purchase precisely because it shies away from the extreme idea of an intentional Jewish plot and thus is able to appeal to wider sections of the right. Broadening our scope further, the outlines of white extinction theory are visible in the 'stranger in our own lands' narrative peddled by parts of the conservative right.

What is the experience of these conspiracies like? A feeling of unstoppability (also a wider hallmark of antisemitic theories) marks out white extinction theory from others such as QAnon, where the 'great awakening' – a moment of redemption – is always just around the corner. The glacial pace of demographic change produces, paradoxically, a feeling of immense urgency: we have to act *now* before it becomes entirely unstoppable. Patriotic Alternative's website hosts a countdown to the day on which white British people will supposedly become a minority in the UK. The ticking of the huge and alarming seconds obscures that this purported event is still – at the soonest – 45 years away.

This conspiracy, like many others, starts out focused on particular events and spirals into an all-encompassing fight for survival. The story of the clash of increasingly general abstraction is also visible in the transformation of ideology on the extreme right. The far right's thinking since the Second World War has become more and more condensed – such that it can be 're-expanded' in any number of ways, to fit a huge variety of occasions – into a simplistic Manichaean struggle between 'the System' and 'the Order' (in the terminology of *The Turner Diaries*, for example),[44] a mythic antagonism that remains prominent today.

What will come to pass if the far right does not act? The apocalypse. The apocalypse, for the most part, is a kitsch idea, of extreme generality. In the most banal versions, people of colour form a permanent voting block against 'white interests'; in the most extreme, metaphysical race war breaks out and white people are exterminated. The chain from this proposition to preemptive murder becomes obvious. If the apocalypse is just around the corner, it means there is no longer anything left to lose, which makes necessary – or finally allows – the genocide of the far right's enemies.

ANTI-SEMITISM

There is always anti-semitism. Anti-semitism is a theory apparently open to almost any data: the insularity of Jewish communities, just as much as their openness, is taken as further evidence, for the antisemite, of the conspiracy. And, like all the most dangerous conspiracies, the lack of evidence is taken as evidence for it. While *The Protocols of the Elders of Zion*, a notorious forgery, outlines a very specific plan for world domination, the openness of antisemitism allows it to explain more or less any phenomena, at more or less any scale. 'Cultural Bolshevism' or 'Judeo-Bolshevism' and later 'Cultural Marxism' are terms used to designate the supposed programmatic force behind large-scale social changes. They are wildly different at times, but each variation holds several things in common, perhaps most importantly a spectral quality, in which the purported Jewish conspiracy "is considered to stand behind phenomena, but not to be identical with them."[45]

Anti-semitism never left the far-right, but it has become a prominent marker of distinction between two tendencies: civic nationalism and ethnonationalist. It is difficult to overstate just how often the latter blames Jews for the many and various ills of society. Jews incite urban disorder through the mainstream media (which they control) and by funding organisations like Black Lives Matter; they degrade Western masculinity through their control of the porn industry, and they control geopolitics through the financial system. The motivation for this seemingly endless mendacity is often left unexplained. Of course, if there is a belief in immutable racial characteristics (almost universal on the far-right) then one is not really required. There is no motivation beyond Jews *acting in their nature*. Such is the argument, for example, of the elaborate scientific racism of Kevin MacDonald.

What does antisemitism provide for the people who believe in it? For those on the far right who imagine the fundamental unit of politics to be race, the lack of cohesive white consciousness, and, indeed, the innumerable really-existing conflicts between white people, require explanation. Anti-semitism in the 'Soros-funding' mode becomes a way of explaining why it is that white people join in with protests against police violence against black people. One of the key findings in Michael Mann's book *Fascists* is that the Nazis were people who found the class conflict of 1920-30s Germany distasteful.[46] They instead wanted to transcend it and re-establish the unity of the German people. 'The Jew' then becomes everything that frustrates the process of making this transcendent unity, namely, both politics and class conflict themselves. Even more abstractly, antisemitism is the result of *anger at the existence of politics itself*: the fury that the community of white people, which in the racist's mind should be unified, turns out to be divided against itself. The Jews, in the contemporary period, by often, confusingly, *appearing to be white*, represent the minimal foundational distinction that constructs all political communities, with their unity and dividedness. The Jews, in antisemitic thought, are they who enforce the constitution of politics as such: as a broken unity.

One should be careful here of giving an overly-clever view of what anti-semitism contains. In an important fragment at the end of *Dialectic of Enlightenment*, Adorno and Horkheimer write "One of the lessons of the Hitler period is the stupidity of cleverness. How many were the expert arguments with which Jews dismissed the likelihood of Hitler's rise, when it was already as clear as daylight."[47] As Adorno and Horkheimer say, in the pleasure of mindless violence against Jews, "the rational island sinks beneath the flood."[48]

FROM APOCALYPSE TO EXTERMINATIONIST ENVIRONMENTALISM

Michael Barkun categorises conspiracy theories into three types: event conspiracies, system conspiracies and super conspiracies. Event conspiracies explain a particular happening, often with reference to a deep and complex network of actors. System conspiracies discuss broad patterns of events, explained as the operations of a particular group of people. In super-conspiracies, multiple conspiracies are linked together hierarchically and in a nested fashion, and the world is seen as controlled by a distant but all-powerful evil agent who decides the outcomes of lesser conspiracies.[49]

We are going to add two other important dimensions to the classification of conspiracies: the depth of who is implicated and the clarity of the referent. These are important, we think, because they tell you about the politicisation of a conspiracy theory. The deeper and broader the conspiracy goes – the more it expresses itself in everyday action, or in ways that are entirely secret even to those who want to prevent it – the more it seems that only a heroic act of social cleansing can eliminate such a conspiracy. What must be done to overturn the conspiracy is therefore quite different – as different as a reactionary preference for an imagined past world and the call for a total social revolution under fascism.

Apocalypticism – although it may seem like it *literally couldn't get any worse* – isn't actually the most extreme form of conspiratorial thinking. While it has an immense breadth, it sometimes lacks depth. Deep conspiracies concern the entirety of the social body, all the way down into its most intimate details: the chemicals that flow through your body, people's individual preferences, and, most importantly, the very ability to discern conspiracy itself. For example, the conspiracy theory that the government is putting stuff in your water is less extreme than the one that people enjoy eating soy. In the former, the government is your enemy.

In the latter, everything and everyone is degenerate. You can imagine the extremity that might be needed to escape such a condition. The conspiracist thinks they need not just opposition to a particular group but a complete phoenix-like burning and resurrection of society.

What is striking is that the far right almost never encounters a new event. What it encounters instead is each new event as a mere continuation of an existing conspiracy, modulated so as to accommodate (and retrospectively predict) whatever has just happened. This is how an event that started in Wuhan, China could be understood *both* as a Jewish conspiracy *and* as an attack on imagined Jewish global domination: both were existing narratives, and the COVID-19 pandemic merely an extension of what was already imagined. It can be placed on either side of the grand conflict. In 2021, the apocalypse *actually is* around the corner. Climate systems breakdown, global pandemics, imminent and ongoing financial crises, increasing antibiotic resistance, and a host of other potential calamities threaten the reproduction of human society on Earth. The far right are unlikely to be able to deal with climate breakdown, except as a function of what they *already* think. We will return to this in our chapter on ecofascism.

For now, let's turn to the production of trusted faces from this hell of noisy information and their propagation of conspiracy as a tool for constructing that most banal of objects: the personal brand.

CONSPIRACY THEORY

THE SWARM AND
THE INFLUENCER

Before the internet, fascists were mostly organised into parties: hierarchical organisations with rigid command structures, a clearly delineated membership and a tendency towards a consistent ideological line, disseminated by the leadership to the rank and file. By 2010, the fascist party, long showing signs of wear, seemed to be conclusively over. Although we will discuss the possibility of its re-emergence in another form in chapter 7, New Organisational Forms, for now let us examine its wreckage, and specifically what has fallen out of it. On the one hand, those people who might have previously joined parties now instead become online audiences or self-identifying members of technically memberless street movements. We call the form these people now take, particularly online, 'the swarm'. On the other hand, those who would have been organisers for parties instead became what we call 'far-right influencers'. As it has evolved, the swarm has acted as a recruitment tool, organisational space, and a means to attack enemies of the far right. In their turn, influencers have built careers leveraging it. This chapter will explore the former, then the latter, and then – most importantly – their complex and frequently antagonistic relationship.

THE SWARM

Boomer QAnon conspirators, savvy identitarian marketeers, blackpilled fashwave SIEGE posters, sameposting bot farmers, imageboard raiders, 'content cucks', forced memers, ethnonationalist livestream chatters, ironically sincere trolls, serial self-indebting superchat donors, furtive lurkers, Islamophobic football ultras, racist Daily Mail commenters, laddish Tommy Robinson acolytes, paid Russiagate trolls, wojak meme auctioneers, cottagecore tradwife instagrammers, suspiciously enthusiastic probable cops, shitposters of all kinds, last-resort neo-Nazi web admins, spiteful MRA forum posters, the groyper army, the hacker known as 4chan, fascist self-help gurus, antifa instigators, Wotansvolk Christian-blamers, plausibly deniable media outlets, Facebook group beginners, Nicker nationalists, Esoteric Hitlerist Telegram channel spammers, Quora question derailers, mewing evangelists, sun and steel weightlifting promoters, MMA fightclub organisers, onion link access explainers, obvious CIA glowposters, Handsome Thursday pinups, mods lax and arbitrary, neoreactionary blogpost bores and your friend of a friend way too deep into antivax: the swarm has many heads.

There are connections and disconnections between all these forces: some interact daily and develop broad alliances, others exist in their own deeply segmented bubbles. Volatility and permeability give the swarm life, but can also lead to ruin. What gives the swarm coherence? It has almost no conventional political form. It's the sum of those actors whose online postings spread far-right ideas, or which sustain an ecosystem in which those ideas become more likely to spread. It's not a singular object – no strategy guides it – yet from the swarm emerges almost everything in this book. Like a diffuse cloud of trillions of tiny bugs, its nebulous buzz focuses only occasionally and ad hoc, but sometimes it can overwhelm its targets, before dispersing back into indistinction.

The swarm is not distinct from the rest of life online. Its internet-use is highly vernacular. Swarm members participate in parallel to their normie activities on other platforms, in between shitposting in the lads groupchat and scrolling through Instagram. Because of this, the tactics themselves, for the most part, seem scarcely worth mentioning: making and circulating memes, videos, podcasts, groups, making private spaces and public posts. These activities, novel in 2010, had become standard by the time of Trump's first election campaign.

It is impossible, nevertheless, to talk about the swarm as a far-right entity without discussing the alt-right. Although now in a state of decline, the alt-right was the most significant instantiation of the swarm to date. It went through a number of iterations, increasingly lacking centralised structure. While prominent figures wielded, at the start, a degree of sway, there were no foundational texts, no events, no universally shared ideas, to give it a permanent direction.

The first iteration – which we will discuss in the chapter on The Right's Intellectuals – was related to paleoconservatism. The second, from 2015-17, operated mostly in relation to the Trump campaign. It possessed, for a time, a genuine sense of countercultural liveliness and produced enduring memes still used on the far right and, indeed, well beyond it. Vitality obsolesced leadership. Andrew Anglin, founder of 'The Daily Stormer', a website named after a Nazi newspaper, wrote in 2016 that "the movement is, at this point, entirely leaderless […] The mob is the movement."[50] Everyone suddenly seemed subsumed within it, from David Duke to advocates of terrorism to Milo Yiannopolous.

This subsumption – like its self-partitioning into 'alt-right' and 'alt-lite' – seemed unreal. This was mostly a function of its novel features: its scale, its destruction of the stratified internet, and its ability to repartition digital space. The three are linked. The scale and speed of posting meant content that would normally have been reserved for 4chan ('the asshole of the internet') and other imageboards could also appear, in glossier form, on YouTube, Facebook, and even the hated Reddit (which later became a major organising hub). It appeared on these websites *as a way of making trouble* – partitioning and repartitioning these platforms, splitting them up into evolving fronts in an ongoing culture war, the far-right side of which was obviously the more impressive, the more radically disinhibiting. Thus, it came to dominate what was significant about these platforms; it became even the image of what was on the internet as a whole. From the mid-2000s to the mid-2010s, the anonymous spaces of the internet were colonised by large social media companies. The rise of the alt-right was linked to the fight by users of online imageboards to keep the cultural power of the internet anonymous, and to do so through making what is found there most impossible to enjoy or affirm for normies: Nazism.

The coalescence of tactics into the swarm, and the emergence of a distinct cultural form of online swarm-activism had an early moment in the now almost mythological events of Gamergate. Here, male gamers felt that their distinctly male space – gaming – was being intruded upon. This event fired the starting gun on a frenetic period of productive aggression that continued until Trump's election and beyond. Klaus Theweleit wrote of the production of male space as integral to the production of fascist desire in the aftermath of the First World War. The war, which had thrown men together, could be juxtaposed to the "slimey bourgeois mire" of civil society afterwards. The contemporary male spaces of online gaming, football fandom, and anonymous online trolling are farcical, pale imitations of this earlier male space in the trenches, but the dynamics and group processes within are not entirely alien. These spaces were distinct from the bourgeois spaces of controlled and polite expression increasingly prominent on the internet in the years leading up to 2016 (Facebook, Twitter, LinkedIn).

The alt-right in its second iteration, unlike other more established movements, almost entirely lacked shared beliefs. Instead, what circulated between its disparate parts was a set of tactics for online action. As the election approached, these tactics took on a mythic stature: 'meme magic' became a catch-all term for what the alt-right could do. While almost never seriously attacking anyone to their right, the alt-right nevertheless fed off increasingly aggressive and confident attacks on the Republican party as well as the movements for social justice whose outrage at Trump provided amusement. When publicly known neo-Nazis did enter or appear to support the movement, disavowal of them was staged ironically or not given at all. Because of the decentralised structure, accusations of racism, usually denied vehemently when aimed at the Republicans, were ignored, or even affirmed, but, either way, almost never had anyone to stick to.

This combination of highly concentrated organising spaces and completely autonomous tendencies in which each group accepted the other as brothers-in-arms, created a tactical flexibility that incentivised innovation. If your meme, or campaign, or photoshopped image has the potential to be taken up *en masse* by the swarm, to suddenly matter in a real way, then staying up all night obsessively tweaking an image becomes a worthwhile activity. How could you be a loser if your content is retweeted by Donald Trump Jr? How could you be insignificant if all these liberals are so triggered?

Despite the chaos, entrance into the alt-right required a kind of discipline. The rote invocation on imageboards for new users to 'lurk moar' is a command to learn the tropes and motifs that, used correctly, will mark you as no one in particular – simply another frequency in the buzzing of the swarm. To be anonymous is not to be nobody; instead, in the swarm, "an anonymous somebody"[51] acts. As Marc Tuters has written: "we might thus characterize the deep vernacular web as a *mask culture* in which individual identity is effaced by the totemic deployment of memes."[52] Anonymous activity online can only rarely be traced back to a real-world body, but the bodies of the actors are deeply involved: they get to feel the exhilarating power and libidinal thrill of communicating suffering by causing it.

This anonymity also makes you uncountable. While it has long been standard activist practice to inflate the attendance of street demonstrations after the fact, on the internet inflation happens in real time. Making thousands of bots simultaneously send out the same or subtly different messages, or simply having a couple of different browsers open at once: inflation can be both highly advanced and stunningly low tech. It is still not clear how many people were involved in the alt-right at its height.

However, none of these tactics was to last forever. The hoped-for revolution in the Republican party failed to manifest, as its corporate wing moved to ameliorate whatever populist bent Trump had brought. To be sure, the Trump administration's policies were racist, but it was not enough –

indeed, likely could never have been enough for a movement that was rapidly radicalising. In so far as Trump's campaign had been galvanizing, his perceived betrayal deflated enthusiasm and, perhaps more crucially for a movement built on speed, slackened participation. The Unite the Right rally at Charlottesville, a public outing of the movement on a global stage, was disastrous, and the movement split. After 2017, the secrecy of one part deepened, and so too did the mytho-aesthetic character of online fascist organising. Ideas expressed exclusively through memes and symbols become increasingly prominent. Impotent to produce substantial change on a national scale, and with the novelty of meme warfare wearing off, fractions of the swarm moved towards greater esotericism and obfuscation. Others moved towards extreme violence.

Deplatforming by anti-fascists was supplemented by that of corporate platform owners and Facebook accounts, Twitter profiles and YouTube channels were shuttered. An extremification process of smaller, more radical groups moving from platform to platform took over. This extremification process concerns groups (detailed in chapter 8 on Deadly Violence) but here we will ask instead: on an individual level, how does one get drawn into the swarm? Online activity fractures people, even more so than they already were to start with. The functions of the swarm are not interested, however, in these fractured people, but only in their most violent and aggressive parts. To these parts it gives voice, and has no need of the rest; however, for the swarm to begin to operate on people, the most intensely violent thoughts and ideas must be first couched in a shared language – ironic, like everything else online. Sharing content is the foundation of the social internet today. The swarm thus allows for you to join in without much thought: 'knowing the party line' is simply a matter of understanding the purpose and effect of a few simple memes. Further, participating in the swarm is a significantly more variable and fun experience than political activity in its traditional form. It requires no attendance at tedious meetings and no stable or long-term commitment. You can participate by posting a single comment from your personal account on YouTube, or you can participate by researching and writing tactical manuals on 'best meme practice' over the course of years. Because of this, the swarm can operationalise all manner of people with hugely variable levels of commitment.

This quickly led to the dissolution of the swarm when it no longer excited frisson in its participants. Participants always were, for the most part, engaged in other things; when the swarm is no longer exciting, breaking away from it is a matter of simply closing a tab. This lack of dense connections for most of its members leads to huge variability in capacity, appearing at some moments to be little more than a few hundred fanatics and at others to contain hundreds of thousands of members. Thus, the content (memes), the organisational form (flexible, variable participation), the form of practice (online sharing of content), and the underlying subjective forms of internet use (fractured personalities with sporadic and transitory interests) are all linked.

This looseness of ties has other implications. In the past, the radicals that exploded from far-right movements often needed to be disavowed for the sake of organisational survival. Group members would act out, say outrageous things or, in extreme cases, kill people, and be expelled from the group as a 'bad apple'. This is no longer the case. The online swarm, although it goes under semi-coherent banners, essentially has no organisational structure to reproduce, so its moments of radicalism and deadly violence are only loosely connected to more prominent individuals. In the past, more radical members could sometimes be constrained from acting out their violent fantasies by pressure from the organisations they would damage if they did so. This is the well-known tactic of the Southern Poverty Law Center, which has bankrupted various extreme-right organisations by bringing civil cases for the actions of errant members. In the online swarm, this is no longer possible. Terrorists can act without the online group coming under fire for it.[53]

FAR-RIGHT INFLUENCERS

The swarm is the roiling maelstrom from which far-right politics now emerges. It has usually been understood as headless, an effect of the network model undermining more centralised organisations. But even in the decentralised or sometimes distributed network of the swarm, certain nodes remain indispensable. For these more significant nodes, it is not command that they centralise, but command's substrate: attention. This is how an ostensibly decentralised form like the swarm came to push celebrities to the fore of the far right even more than before. In this section, it is these nodes we are concerned with, whose *appearance* as figures distinct from the swarm is an aspect of their power. Figurehead, spokesperson, cheerleader, take generator, shibboleth definer, hate focuser, swarm noise compressor, alliance maker, radicalisation funneler, vicarious emotion feeler, network densifier, debate participant, fundraiser, personal advisor, performative criticism taker, perfect victim, mythic lib owner: the influencer has many roles.

Their emergence from the swarm is inherently full of tensions: too distinct and they become detached from the group that gives them power; too indistinct and they lose traction, dissolving back into the swarm. Their relationship with the swarm is therefore, ultimately, tense, and their status relies on their ability to give it continual stimulation and articulation. They are the key nodes of what Steve Bannon has called "a politics of mobilisation", less and less concerned with the organisation of a coherent group with a stable agenda, and more and more concerned with the incitement of feeling. Far-right influencers are the main dealers in a culture of dosing on outrage. Novelty plays a huge part in the question of how outraged someone can feel; however, only a very small number of topics really hit the mark. Thus, novelty comes not from broadening out the politics to other issues, but from stating more and more extreme positions on a select few fixations. The swarm's conventionalism is the conventionalism *of* extremism, a progressive narrowing of focus. If influencers stray even a little too far from its narrow beliefs, it turns off. Between these two demands – the demand that you say something unique and the demand that you stay with what everyone already thinks – lies the thin path of the successful influencer, but it sets in motion a pattern of radicalisation between the swarm and the influencer that frequently runs afoul of the platforms on which it depends.

The pressure of conventionality, without the pressure of novelty, can lead to the redundancy of the influencer entirely. Usually, the influencer provides for the swarm a degree of articulation of their politics. They make explicit what their members believe but are unable to say for themselves. Too clear, or too general, an ideology and the influencers become unimportant, as we argue took place in the 2020 'statue defender' protests in the UK. When the politics consists entirely in defending the statue of Winston Churchill, influencers lose one of their main functions. Churchill is 'our boy'. Everyone knows it. Influencers were no longer needed to articulate the underlying politics and so were discarded.

Some individuality is thus essential for each influencer. But this is an individuality built not on ideas, but on an affective connection to the swarm. In terms of the emotional motor of far-right politics, far-right leadership today follows rather than leads. It does so through sensing and orienting the mood of the swarm, developing an instinct for its movements, learning its underlying transformations of emotion, and confidently embodying its desires. Compared to the fascist leaders of the past, who mythically embodied the nation, today, in our much more atomised world, it is more often a question of who can appear most to be your friend.

This affective power raises the stakes of radicalisation for influencers. Because they must seem to be *really present,* and therefore authentic, to maintain their power, influencers have vastly more skin in the game than their swarm followers. Radicalisation thus has very different stakes for the individuals who appear on the screen, whose individuality is particular and whose presentation has a necessary consistency, and for the anonymous swarm who rarely need to appear as themselves. As participation in far-right movements declines (as it periodically does), these highly particularised and 'authentic' influencers are less likely to be able to exit the movement. Thus, radicalisation often burns their ability to exit the far right cleanly, whereas it has very few consequences for swam members, a difference that intensifies the tension between the demands of the two. One of the main tensions between the swarm and influencer lies in the former's thirst for more and more radical statements, and the latter's resistance to them.

This proof-of-authenticity is demanded the most for women influencers, whose commitment to the movement is always seemingly most in doubt. Brittany Sellner's (nee Pettibone) stereotypical 1950s feminine presentation – 'tradwifing' – is perhaps typical of women far-right influencers. She married Martin Sellner, leader of Generation Identity, in 2019. Tradwives like Pettibone occupy an uncomfortable place in white nationalist movements, which are both dominated by men and are riddled with misogyny. Women influencer's radicalisation can be marked not by more extreme statements but by their retreat from politics: Lauren Southern, who was attacked by some on the far right for failing to live up to her supposed ideals of femininity by not having a child herself, took a year off after the release of her documentary into the migration crisis, had said child, and returned.

For platforms, radicalisation beyond a certain point is *verboten*. To become an influencer thus requires the ability to produce content that is acceptable to three distinct audiences: the swarm, potential recruits, and the platform. The influencer must not be so radicalised by the swarm's demand for more edgy content that they get deplatformed. The extremist's dilemma – between greater openness and greater security – is transformed from a dilemma inside a single group (as it was for, say, the National Front) into a tension between the swarm and the influencers.

Influencers can, however, present themselves as faking it in one very specific way: they can winkingly disguise their own radicalism. Indeed, this very obvious disguising of extreme beliefs (for example, antisemitism) can seem to the audience like a shared secret: a mark of a personal connection. In doing so, influencers can cultivate cults of personal loyalty.

Mark Collett of Patriotic Alternative finessed this style in 2020, splitting his content across platforms according to its radicalism. Collett's videos on YouTube, with its 'three strikes' policy, are carefully scripted and checked before publication in order to stick to the letter of the terms of service. On smaller platforms with fewer restrictions, such as Dlive and BitChute, his antisemitism is much more explicit. Presence over a range of platforms also provides a level of built-in redundancy for influencers.

Being unique is also necessary for one of the most effective ways of densifying the network of influencers as a whole: public livestreamed debates, known as 'internet bloodsports'. In these online debates between two or more influencers, the swarm pitches in, in the comments section, rooting for their guy. These bloodsports simultaneously fulfil a bunch of functions: they connect disparate groups of the swarm through the meeting of multiple audiences; they produce hugely extended video content; and they provide the sense of a vibrant, diverse, intellectual culture. The constellation of content creators and accounts forms a self-supporting network with a high degree of audience crossover: if one creator is banned from a particular platform they can fall back to another outlet, while fellow creators help reestablishment by directing their followers to the new outlet. We also cannot discount the visceral excitement common across the internet of seeing someone you do not like getting owned, or watching them post cringe, or picking on the losers within your side.

Bloodsports allows for members of the swarm to become influencers, a possibility that must forever be held open. It is through becoming an influencer that at least some of the hopeless-feeling men of the far right will come to feel important. In terms of their composition of social capital, far-right influencers present themselves as the stark opposite of their audience. However, it cannot be made too easy for the swarm to become financially viable through influencing – being an influencer is, after all, lucrative.

Money is an important part of swarm-influencer dynamics. Although some influencers have money from elsewhere – rich patrons, or regular jobs – many rely on audience donations. The system of superchats and normalisation of a political tipping culture has allowed for the production of 'professional racists' who live entirely off donations (whereas no one will pay to attend a demonstration). Thus, the financial incentives pull more strongly towards audience production and less towards street actions. In times of ascendency for the far right this can be exceptionally lucrative. In times of a reduction in activity, less so: influencers, who are more tied to the far right by virtue of what they have said, scrape around and compete for the last bits of money available. As participation declines, they are left in a lurch, and must often move further to the right, where the more radical tend to stick around for longer, and, importantly, give more money.

In moments of decline, motivating and sustaining activity and presenting things as more hopeful than they actually are, are important skills. In the Telegram chats of the far-right, stopping the tendency towards blackpilling – posting depressing, pessimistic content that makes its audience believe there is nothing to do but commit sporadic violence – takes on an existential importance. On the livestreams and videos around which the swarm congregates, there are constant exhortations to 'whitepill' instead of blackpill, to raise racial consciousness and *do something* rather than fall further and further into inactivity and despair.

More generally, in the post-Charlottesville world, as the less radical influencers fell away, or were sucked back into mainstream Trumpism, the more extreme ones doubled down as they competed for reduced supporter donations. Mostly, however, they have struggled. In recent years, founder of the Daily Stormer Andrew Anglin has been in hiding from multiple civil judgments on his campaigns of harassment. The Daily Shoah, the most prominent podcast of the alt-right, which once commanded significant audiences and spawned a network of fascist shows, was deplatformed by podcast providers and has retained only a niche following, although its influence hasn't collapsed completely. After Charlottesville, the style of mainstream journalism keen to trade on the novelty of 'dapper' white nationalists such as Richard Spencer also waned, as the movement's deadly consequences became evident even to the least perceptive liberal. Some, like Spencer, were rejected by the swarm themselves: failure decapitates the movement.

This capacity of the swarm – to be weaponised against its leaders, particularly its less explicitly radical ones – has been clearest in the case of 'Groyping', a tactic that sprang up around white nationalist content creator Nick Fuentes and his attempts to influence the mainstream conservative movement. 'Groypers' made interventions at the rallies of Turning Point USA, an astroturfed conservative movement, where besuited white nationalists asked leading questions on Zionism, tolerance of homosexuality, and other issues of importance for the far right. The aim is to expose the contradictions within conservatism and humiliate the speaker by tying them up in knots. The intention for Groypers is to open the (mostly) one-way trap door from conservatism to fascism. The tactic is similar to one used by The League of Empire Loyalists, a group established in the 1950s in defence of British empire, who practised the same kind of interventions at right wing or otherwise establishment events.

This tactic has oscillated between physical and online space. When the tactic migrated to the UK, Groypers turned to crashing popular centre-right phone-in radio programs. In the UK, during the COVID-19 lockdown, calls into talk radio stations such as Talksport and LBC – particularly to hosts with right-wing audiences – became a tactic for promoting ethnonationalism. In December 2020, Labour leader Keir Starmer was ambushed by white nationist yoga teacher Jody Swingler on an LBC phone-in show. There, code words for white extinction theories such as 'demographic decline' and 'anti-white racism' are used as talking points for interventions within the right. The arrival of the UK Groypers signals a shift in the UK far right as the politics of Tommy Robinson and UKIP is challenged by a more extreme iteration.

Two people who have combined and mastered all these various functions, albeit in totally different ways, and who have gone through a similar cycle to the influencer strata as a whole (at time of writing, rapidly waning in influence), are Tommy Robinson and 'Q' of QAnon. It is to these two that we now turn.

TOMMY ROBINSON

The career of Tommy Robinson illustrates the relationship between swarms and influencers. During the 2010s, Robinson displayed an impressive capacity for reinvention, and thus became an influencer with a remarkable degree of longevity. First as the founder and leader of the EDL, then a sudden and unconvincing conversion to think-tank anti-extremism, then as a 'citizen-journalist', and, finally, as professional political martyr, Robinson has been a protean figure. Attendance at far-right protests in the UK is highly variable, and for a long time was directly related to Robinson's support.

One line of attack on Tommy Robinson is to point out that his real name is in fact Stephen Christopher Yaxley-Lennon.

This oft-repeated gesture of unmasking implicitly argues: 'This man is not the figure of truth-telling authenticity that he pretends to be. He is, in fact, a banal man with an awkward name. He's a petty-bourgeois tanning salon owner from Luton who has been convicted of mortgage fraud and who stole his name from a famous local football hooligan.' But this unmasking gesture misses the point of the performance. 'Authenticity' for influencers, while essential, actually means something quite different from personal truthfulness. Instead, they are embodiments of a movement's self-image, an image that is simultaneously powerful and uncertain.

Robinson has been careful to mask his racism. He repeatedly demands that his interlocutors quote back to him the words he is supposed to have said that are racist. Rather, his racism has been a matter of persistent emphasis. He reports near-exclusively on 'Muslim grooming gangs' (groups of Muslim men who groomed and sexually assaulted girls in Rotherham) and Islamic terrorism. However, sometimes he slips up, describing British Muslims as "enemy combatants who want to kill you, maim you and destroy you" and declaring that refugees are "raping their way through the country".[54]

It was through joining the far-right news site Rebel Media and his subsequent re-emergence as a confrontational 'citizen journalist' that he found his greatest success. Most famous from his time in this guise of 'citizen journalism' was his livestream from outside a court in Leeds, where a group of Muslim men were on trial for the sexual exploitation of children. There were reporting restrictions on the trial, making both Robinson's reporting from outside and his attempts to film the defendants illegal. The livestream Robinson took outside the court is typical of his presentation style. He is both the revealer of information and its keeper. He informs us that he will know the verdicts of the trial but he will not be allowed to report on it. He lets us know that something is happening off camera but not what. At the end of the video he is arrested. None of this is sufficient occasion for Robinson to film anything other than himself. In this world, Robinson is all that matters, and that he purports to see something corrupt, says that something terrible is going on, is all the confirmation his audience needs of what they already believe.

Robinson had tried this stunt before: mere weeks earlier, he had been warned by a judge for contempt of court, and told that a repeat offence would lead to him being sent to prison. Predictably, when he attempted the stunt again this was exactly where he was sent, triggering the #FreeTommy movement. At his peak, Robinson had amassed hundreds of thousands of followers across his social media accounts, a popularity further increased by this transformation into his last role, that of a political martyr.

There's a risk of overstating Robinson's strategic genius here. Just because being sent to prison was lucrative for him, doesn't mean that it was planned. Although his personal profile was raised dramatically, in his absence his various deputies turned out to be highly incompetent (typical of the far right generally, but perhaps particularly so in the post-party era of the influencers), and by August 2019, the street movement had dissolved into nothing. He had lost his digital reach as well. After his near-comprehensive deplatforming, he is left with his own website, which he rarely writes for, a channel on the messaging app Telegram, a profile on the Russian social media site VK, and one on the alternative 'free speech' platform Parler. None of these has nearly the reach of his previous platforms.

Although the swarm depends on influencers, it never depends on a *particular* influencer, at least not for a sustained period of time. The demise of one is accommodated within the swarm/influencer ecosystem. Sometimes, the swarm turns on an influencer, especially those who seem to be moderating their views. Sometimes, an influencer rejects the swarm, and sometimes an influencer loses their hold over the swarm, as was the case with Tommy Robinson. Just as in the case of the swarm, the lack of an institutional form produces both rapid rises and rapid falls. His demise provided an opportunity for other influencers to take up space that was previously unavailable in the UK. Most prominent amongst these is Mark Collett and the coterie of content creators surrounding Patriotic Alternative.[55]

Q

'Q' of QAnon is the most important influencer today; they are also the most unusual. Someone claiming to have Q-level security clearance in the US government, close to Trump, and reporting on his struggle against the deep state. Their authenticity, which is deeply felt by their audience, is not their own, but is the authenticity of Trump, or even that of the US itself, as conceived in the minds of their patriotic and myopic audience. We might say that in the case of Q, all the various demands placed on influencers are suspended: their ability to conjure a world of meaning makes them impervious to these pressures. In short, the religious aspects of Q remove them from the economy of 'takes' and from the necessity even of coherence, even of continuing to exist. As Q has steadily posted less, and more lackadaisically, the culture around them has splintered and developed almost entirely on its own. In this, Q has become the spawn for hundreds of smaller scholastic influencers, whose power consists in their ability to make Q make sense. Rather than being in competition with others, Q requires this whole industry to function at all.

Q is some strange transformation of the joke into the brand into the religion, but such conditions are extremely rare. More common are the tensions between those with faces and those without, the pressures of banality and extremism, the grift and inter-influencer competition. Sitting somewhat above these changes is another form of articulation of roughly the same politics, albeit less subject to the churn of interest and fashion: intellectuals. It is here that far-right ideas become most clearly articulated, but at the same time, it is here that they frequently lose touch with their audiences altogether. We turn to them now.

THE RIGHT'S INTELLECTUALS

I t is sometimes said that classical fascism was anti-intellectual. But like any ideological movement, it did have its thinkers. Swathes of European intellectuals, impressed by Mussolini and the fascist experiment more generally, not only affirmed the project but were enthusiastic participants within it. In power, however, fascism relegated philosophy well below force. Intellectuals, although crucial to the formation of fascism, were rapidly marginalised within the wider movement, and naked propagandists pillaged their work for simpler formulations. Some anti-intellectualism was also internal to fascist intellectualism itself. Confronted with the discursive complexity of modernity, as George Valois expressed, the answer of fascism was to 'raise the sword':

> "The bourgeois brandishing his contracts and statistics:
> – two plus three makes. . . .
> – Nought, the Barbarian replies, smashing his head in."[56]

A recent book on the thinkers of the 'Radical Right' found less sympathy for Nazism than Italian fascism among its classical thinkers, Julius Evola, Oswald Spengler, and Ernst Jünger. The problem with Nazism, however, wasn't always that it was too extreme, but that it was too plebeian. Evola was critical of fascism 'from the Right'; Spengler was too fond of the German aristocracy to accept National Socialism's mass form; and Jünger's sympathies were conservative rather than radical nationalist.[57] These thinkers of the right positioned themselves against undisciplined mass movements and – putting it very broadly – in favour of the aristocratic, the elite. In the Aryanism of Arthur de Gobineau, and in the 'Elite Theory' of the Italian school, eliteness is necessarily a minority quality. But substantial fractions of nations could be *made* spiritually aristocratic through submission, through sacrifice.

Another tendency is exemplified by Martin Heidegger's contributions to 'homeland studies', particularly his essay 'Why I Stay in The Provinces'. This essay, although it does not summon a boundless elite, summons a highly bounded – and therefore deep and true – eliteness from the very commonest of particularities. Another tendency still was exemplified by Carl Schmitt, whose theory of politics relied on the existence of an almost theological elite who could make the decisive constitutive gesture of politics itself: the sovereign who could declare the exception to the normal functioning of law.

The far right today also has many intellectuals. Perhaps because extra-state violence is now more taboo in politics, the far right now is less vehemently opposed to its own philosophical justification. Nevertheless, these movements still often conceive of themselves as an elite. The construction of this elite takes place differently across the various distinct groupings of right intellectuals: the soft right (familiar from book shops across the world), the groups and journals whose work consists of pseudointellectual musings on race and IQ, 'very online' affirmations of masculinism, the first alt-right, the European New Right's heirs in Duginism, the strange new face of Neoreaction, various disparate Right Accelerationists, and, at the bottom of the intellectual pile, bleeding into the 'far-right influencers' of the previous chapter, the self-styled intellectuals of podcasts, YouTube and Bitchute.

The right likes to style itself as intellectually insurgent. From Jordan Peterson's bewailing of 'postmodern neo-Marxists' to Sam Harris and Charles Murray's gentlemanly discussion of racial differences in IQ, the style of presentation is similar across the board: this is 'secret knowledge', previously kept from their audiences by nefarious vested interests. In truth, it has been continuously accessible online, in every bookshop, and in the column pages of major newspapers. It styles its enemy – 'wokeness' – as an over-intellectual movement combining precious effeminacy with the hegemonising strong arm of the law. The elite is constituted by those who have resisted this force by being intellectually forthright, honest, and unafraid of their own conclusions. This is a capacious eliteness; anyone who has watched a few YouTube videos can consider themselves a member.

The individualistic 'soft right' thinkers named above are, however, quite different from thinkers on the organised far and fascist right. For the latter, eliteness is almost always related to participation within obscure and exclusive intellectual cultures. Indeed, in some recent iterations, such as in parts of the alt-right and in Patriotic Alternative, there is an almost manic insistence on 'debate'. Matthew Heimbach, for a time one of the most prominent members of the alt-right, reported that, for him, the principal attraction of the Iron March forums, a neo-Nazi website,[58] was its detailed intellectual discussion. These forms of 'intellectual' culture, by connecting the holding of obscure and tendentious beliefs to the self-conception of eliteness, allow for superiority to express itself through membership of subgroups.

The works that interest these latter groups, from Julius Evola to Alexander Dugin to Daniel Friberg, often rely on washy abstractions that paper over the lack of a serious explanatory framework for the world. In the American far right in particular, conspiratorial anti-communism bleeding into antisemitism has often replaced the more nuanced (albeit still conspiratorial and false) accounts of capitalism given by some interwar European fascists. Despite this persistent conjuring of new abstractions, recurring fixations can be teased out of the general unclarity: race science, biological essentialism, selective use of appeals for free speech, narratives of degeneracy and collapse and, ultimately, the naturalisation of hierarchy.

Let us now move rapidly through the various aspects and sub-groups of the intellectual far right, each time asking the question: how do these intellectual trends support the construction of an elite?

THE CONSTRUCTION OF ELITES

Much race and IQ research is supported by the Pioneer Fund, the organisation set up in 1937 towards the end of a wave of enthusiasm for scientific racism in the US. This wave had been highly successful in promoting eugenics, and some of its most prominent members, including those who would go on to form the first board of directors of the Pioneer Fund, praised the Nazis' sterilisation programme. Today, the fund is headed by Richard Lynn, who also sits on the board of *Mankind Quarterly*, one of the principal journals of race science. Its involvement beyond this is shady: recipients of its grants are not required to declare they have received the funding. For this group of far-right intellectuals, apparent adjacency to the mainstream of science (even if their research is widely criticised) is one way of making themselves appear as a cognitive elite. The journal *Intelligence*, otherwise highly respected, has been accused of laundering the reputations of scientific racists by publishing their work.

This concern for prestige is far from universal on the far right. For others, marginality confers and confirms eliteness. Paradoxically, this affirmation of marginality sometimes makes them more available to a wider audience. One such author (his book was self-published anonymously) is the Bronze Age Pervert, or BAP. BAP argues in his *Bronze Age Mindset* that contemporary men are less virile because they are permeated with xenoestrogens: they are 'bugmen'. He argues – through Friedrich Nietzsche – for the creation of a new man.[59] In this, he is not dissimilar to Jack Donnavan, whose hypermasculine *The Way of Men* advocated for a thoroughgoing 'androphilia' as the core of collective pack-based experience.[60] The pair of them share not only a collection of arguments but also an aesthetics. The work is primarily exhortation: to forms of vital life in 'owned space' and to biological masculinism. It is this tension between rational argumentation and the will to overcome this grounding reason through an aesthetic and biological forcefulness that animates this part of the far-right intellectual scene, and links it back to fascist intellectual's anti-intellectualism of the past. Briefly, BAP was a major part of the 'online dissident right', although he wasn't productive enough as a writer for its fast-paced economy of hot takes. Indeed, BAP's principled refusal to submit to the pace of online commentary eventually drove him from relevance, and the intellectual efforts of the 'online dissident right' returned to more modest pursuits.

Such a tension between the speed of online activity and intellectuality was visible in the difference between the first two manifestations of the alt-right. Before it was a crass meme-swarm in the 2016 election, or had emerged as a riotous cacophony of holistic bigotry at Charlottesville, the alt-right thought of itself as an intellectual movement. Richard Spencer was the president of the impeccably grey-sounding National Policy Institute, and mostly operated through AlternativeRight.com, an initiative of the same. There, he published lengthy articles that, in contrast with its contemporaries, did not focus exclusively on race but took in foreign and domestic policy, gender and other subjects that spoke to a more coherent worldview.

When the movement was in its ascendency, these self-styled intellectuals momentarily changed tactics, but in the period of the movement's decline, it has returned to such content, now operating chiefly through the online magazine Radix (founded in 2012), where it assembles leading lights such as Edward Dutton (editor-in-chief of *Mankind Quarterly*) to debate the pressing topics of 2021 like the New Atheist movement.

Similarly broad in its project of addressing all culture from the standpoint of the far right, the long-running Identitarian Ideas conference, organised by the MotPol think tank, brings together international members of the far right to debate and develop their ideas. It is not widely attended: here as for the readers of the alt-right content on Radix, eliteness is imagined through its capacity to provide an apparently integrated cultural system for a select few.

The Identitarian Ideas conference sits in the lineage of the European New Right. It is not the only group to do so. Perhaps more significant, and certainly more shrouded in myth, is Eurasianism and its chief thinker, Alexander Dugin. Dugin – the importance of whom assessments oscillate between 'freelance writer' and 'master strategist of Russian and Trumpian American power' – is also a highly syncretic thinker. His thinking draws from writers of the German Conservative Revolution, from Traditionalists, from the Eurasianists, from Plato, and from fascists. Here, intellectual heft is provided by variety, by the apparent ability to always bring something else in. As below, Dugin affirms an eliteness through obfuscation, as well as through declarations that his work is itself only comprehensible by an elite. Want to be the elite? Declare that you too have mastered Dugin's repertoire of abstractions. Nevertheless, despite this apparently fearsome intellectual armature (or perhaps because of it) his works often end up compressed into what the French writer Emmanuel Carrère has called "the parish bulletins of the European extreme right."[61]

The blogosphere – parish bulletins of the early 21st century – was the founding place for Neoreaction (NRx), a political theory advocating authoritarian monarchical government on the model of the corporation. It describes a system in which a large number of independent city states compete in a semi-open market to provide governance solutions to the world's population, who are given a sole political right: if you don't like it, leave. Go somewhere where you will be treated better. Although there is no particular mechanism that its main proponent, Curtis Yarvin, gives for their selection, the ideal CEOs/monarchs of these city states are very much like the tech CEOs that bestride the globe now. Despite being strictly authoritarian, Neoreaction is nevertheless a form of libertarianism, in pursuit of a small state. The argument: the more authoritarian the state, the smaller it can be.[62] This authoritarianism, which grants the sole right of exit, supporters of NRx imagine, will produce ideal forms of sorting as all demographics are organised back into their fitting polities. What this conception fails to understand is that personality differences are not, broadly, matters of biological givenness (an implicit biological essentialism), but are the product, in part at least, of functional differences produced by political systems themselves. Separation is no answer: differences would simply re-emerge.

Neoreaction is not clearly on the far right as discussed elsewhere in this book. However, we have included it here because it will probably be a major component in the future alloys of far-right thought. Neoreactionaries matter because they can become a way of solving problems in a much larger, more prominent, libertarian movement, through a turn towards political authoritarianism. The arrangement of neoliberalism – democratic political sovereignty defined, and eroded, by the market – is replaced in NRx by an arrangement of authoritarian sovereignty that is made absolute under conditions in which absolute governments are forced to compete. Is the model really so inaccessible from where we currently stand? Might governance, handed over to corporations, not turn increasingly into something quite like this? This position – the 'right of capital' – is also that of the now-atrophied movement called Right Accelerationism, which pegs its hopes to the movement of capital itself, and imagines the process of subsumption of life under capitalism to be the process of a rational – and racialised – sorting.

Given the coming environmental crisis, it is not difficult to imagine that this might be a future increasingly attractive to more conventional right-wingers as well. As the far right looks for ways to scale up again, one of its most important signal changes will be in its relationship to established capital, and this relationship's expression in intellectual components of the far right. In particular, the position it takes with regards to the clash and intermeshing of formal and informal hierarchies constitutive of capitalism will determine to some extent its capacity to return to scale.

Intellectual activity such as NRx can function, and often does, not as the stimulant for mass movements, but as the spur for more diffuse transformations in global power. It is through its intellectuals, who fit in uncomfortably to the movement dynamics discussed elsewhere in this book, that the far right becomes important for this quite different project. This is where the inadequacy we noted above in the case of the Bronze Age Pervert – to become a voice in a movement – becomes a strength, as the longer, slower lessons the far right produces about political power are silently absorbed by existent right-wing power structures. That, however, is for another book.

THE STREET

THE STREET, THE SWARM
AND THE BEDROOM

Fascism has always extolled action. Specifically, it has idealised a vitality that is demonstrated in public space (although, like any radical ideology, it has also dabbled in secrecy). This action is necessarily carried out by real bodies in conflict with the forces that would constrain them: communists, anti-fascists, or the state. In interwar fascism, urban space was central. The metropolitan street was simultaneously a site of commerce, politics and social life. Control of the street therefore meant an imposition of will on this social life. Though Mussolini came to power through technically legal means codified in the Italian constitution, the March on Rome in October 1922 solidified what had already become evident: Mussolini was in charge. Fascism has relied on the physical occupation of the street precisely because it was associated with untrammelled public power. Fascists want to make their superiority unmistakable.

Online, power is fakeable. Hacking, trolling, and swarming are the tactics of actors who *have no right* to be as powerful as they are. On the alt-right, this asymmetrical potency lent the movement a sense of insurgency. But it wasn't enough. Despite the internet – an extension and blurring of public and private space – there remains a pervasive feeling that *the street,* and the ability to exert a will within it, imbues a movement with legitimacy.

The street, however, is a risky space in which doxxing, being punched in the head, boredom, and arrest are all possible. The power of the digital swarm lies in its capacity for sudden anonymous mass action online: raiding a Discord server, publishing the address of a journalist, making a particular meme or phrase trend across a global platform, saturating a comments section with racist invective – and to do all this in relative individual safety. As discussed previously, these are a far cry from taking over the power of the state, but they are not trivial capacities. On the street, this safety is stripped away. As if to fulfil for the umpteenth time in the post-war period Marx's evergreen tragedy/farce dyad, the swarm of chapter 4 has been somewhat less successful when it manifests on the street. Unfamiliar with conventional political action, they have been beset by the same problems previous generations have faced. Anime avatars are replaced with people who, for a time, lose their collective ability to endlessly reproduce content, harass and overwhelm, as well as to exaggerate their numbers. Tedious practical considerations of travel and accommodation combine with the undeniable control the state has over most physical space, as well as the determined physical opposition of anti-fascists. By becoming corporeal, activity within the movement loses its appeal. These movements remain, for all their failures, just as murderous in intention.

None of this is to say that new street movements have not resulted from the digital ferment. There is, in fact, a complex interrelation between digital communities and the street that has existed since the popularisation of the internet. The alt-right and its physical appearance at Charlottesville is the central example but it was not the only one. The waves of UK and European street protest from 2009 all had a foundation in, or were influenced by, a similar style of edgy memes, harassment, and leaderless aggression that were the hallmarks of the alt-right swarm. Here, we explore the 'pisshead nationalism' of the English Defence League (EDL), Democracy Football Lad's Alliance (DFLA) and Free Tommy demonstrations in the UK and the street manifestations of the alt-right from Charlottesville on.

Gone for the most part are the fascist masses, the fascist crowds. Fascism without a homogenous mass is an unusual formation: fascism without leaders even more so. No longer do thousands of uniformed men march in formation through the streets – although exceptions exist, such as the Indian RSS and in Greece, where the now broadly defunct Golden Dawn attempted to reclaim the classic fascist imagery of the street. Largely, however, the imposition of a single aesthetic has failed. In the UK, there has long been a ban on political uniforms. The fascists at Charlottesville were heterogeneous to the point of aesthetic chaos. This change can be linked to the distribution of stunt propaganda. Where, in the past, the mass was displayed in propaganda films distributed by the fascist party (e.g., Reifenstal's *Triumph of the Will*), now only spectacles of disorder and chaos are gripping enough to reliably be passed through the network. This means that a certain kind of aesthetic heterogeneity is a necessary part of the swarm. If political uniforms and marching in formation are less and less achievable – although not gone entirely – far-right crowds are astonishingly homogeneous in other ways. This focus on 'the look' of fascism is not trivial: in fascism the appearance of order-as-such can take precedence over the character of this order. As we will detail in the following chapter, however, in internet aesthetics, order and chaos are intertwined.

PISSHEAD NATIONALISM: FROM THE EDL TO STATUE DEFENDERS

The 2010s saw a new strand of far-right politics come to the fore in the UK, one that rejected traditional political formations such as the party, and relied instead on organic methods of mobilisation – mobilising as the amplification and politicisation of existing group connections. Starting with the English Defence League (EDL) in 2009, through the Democratic Football Lads Alliance (DFLA) and Free Tommy demonstrations, and into the statue defenders of 2020, these groups organised the largest far-right street demonstrations in generations.

These movements are often non-ideological in any explicit sense; they largely would not place themselves within a fascist or far-right tradition. But one does not have to be on the far right or subscribe to a far-right programme to act as the far right. These movements operate around generalised bigotries: Muslims, lefties and other unpatriotic elements. Their rhythm is dictated by national outrages such as terrorism, sexual assault cases, and left-wing protests, towards which, in the protestors' view, the government, journalists and the police, among others, show a despicable indifference. The state is soft. The street movements set out to rectify the injustice.

Far-right organisations today, unable to manifest the social order they crave, instead demand something much more mundane: that the state fulfils its contractual obligations. Across the movementist far right, the police are called upon to the 'do their jobs': prosecute 'paedo rape gangs', sink migrant's boats in the Mediterranean, or declare 'antifa' a terrorist organisation. In part, this is because the contemporary state is in a position of unassailable power, much more so than it was in the early 20th century. Because they have no hope of substantive change, and no imagination for it, in the UK these movements lack a viable kind of future-orientation. They are thus erratic, jumpy.

The demographic that comes on these demonstrations is always there in society at times of crisis (and we have been in a crisis for a decade) – some figures have just learnt to call on it better. These movements have a tendency to fizzle out as the outrage that spurred street action fades or if key influencers begin to lose interest or standing. Since these movements' inception, both participants and influencers have risen and fallen into and out of favour, into and out of engagement, dependent on their ability to be charasmatically stimulated by the issues or their ability to stimulate others.

Some have tried to harness these crowd's power for their own – more conventionally 'political' – ends. A post-referendum UKIP under the leadership of Gerard Batten actively courted the DFLA and Tommy Robinson. They have also attracted derision from other sections of the far right, particularly those in the party tradition, such as Patriotic Alternative, who have sneeringly disdained a lack of ideological coherence and a prevalent culture of alcohol consumption. They call it 'pisshead nationalism'. The term is both indicative of an uncomfortable attitude towards a working class aesthetic and a fairly apt description of movements whose space for doing their politics is the pub as much as the street.

Aside from their generalised bigotry, these street movements' mode of mobilisation is their most salient feature for us. As there are no formal procedures for membership, to 'be a member' is to buy an organisation's merchandise and attend demonstrations, or simply like the relevant Facebook pages and participate in comment threads. Weaker still, membership can be by self-identification. This means the organisation only *really exists* (and therefore is only really accountable) when it's actually on the streets – at the exact point it's flexing its power and the excitement of the moment makes it unconcerned with its image. Their ramshackle appearance – and their lack of interest in changing it – is thus a consequence of their mode of organising.

The EDL and 'Free Tommy'

The EDL came into being rather haphazardly, as a response to a radical Islamist group protesting a procession for returning soldiers. Its direct predecessor, United People of Luton, did not have an organisational framework on which the EDL could build, so instead it turned to the infrastructure it had available: social media and widespread Islamophobia. It relied, as would later movements, on already-existing football firms[63] to make up its base. The network is decentralised rather than fully distributed – it connects existing clumps together.

The power to mobilise this network became, over time, increasingly focused on Tommy Robinson, the EDL's leader. The lack of thick organisation-building, and an over-reliance on Robinson as a figurehead and mobiliser meant that his resignation and denunciation of Nazis within the ranks created a power vacuum. The EDL had its own website and social media accounts, but its followers looked to Robinson for leadership. This mobilisation system was one part existing networks being tied together and one part personal charisma.

Today, the EDL barely exists, although it refuses to fully disappear. The amorphous organisational form and ideology of the EDL came to dominate the UK far right over the course of the next decade and inspired a number of similar 'defence leagues' across Europe. Tommy Robinson's other involvements with street-based movements, most prominently Pegida, came to nothing, in part because they were not mobilised around either existing networks or his charisma.

When Tommy Robinson was sent to prison for disrupting the trial of sexual abusers in 2018, his transformation into a martyr returned him to prominence and triggered the rise of the Free Tommy movement. The more traditionally organised and ideologically defined far right saw Free Tommy as a place to make an intervention. The UK chapter of Generation Identity, usually too small to organise without disruption, felt safe enough to display their flags there. It was also an occasion for members of long dormant groups, such as the neo-Nazi Combat 18, to reappear. UKIP, transformed under Gerrad Batten from a wildly successful metapolitical project for leaving the EU to an all-purpose anti-Muslim vehicle, also appeared to court Tommy Robinson fans. Again, when Robinson was actually sent to prison, his deputies were no replacement, and without him the tenuous alliances fell apart.

Democratic Football Lads Alliance (DFLA)

When the Westminster attacks and the bombing of the Manchester Arena were carried out by Jihadists, killing twenty-eight people, many of them children, there was no longer an EDL to capture the fury and fear they generated. Instead, the Football Lad's Alliance (FLA) was formed. After several large marches, in advance of which they contacted anti-fascists to deny being far right, dissent within them grew. Organisation through informal hierarchies had reached a limit familiar from tensions between the swarm and influencers: the demand of the mass to push for greater radicalism, and the reluctance of figureheads to do so. A breakaway group including, most prominently, Phil Hickin, appended a 'Democratic' to the name, and formed the DFLA.

Much organising for their marches was done on football fan forums or social media (Telegram is only used if you have a relation to the state which is fundamentally adversarial). These sites are hardly the anonymised subterranean spaces of the dark web, but neither are they exactly the 'public sphere' of open Facebook groups or named Twitter accounts. They replicated online the existing structure of offline spaces: true to the group's name, these too were largely communities based around football.

In 2018, the DFLA switched campaign tactics. Deliberately courting a more respectable image than the EDL, and perhaps aware that terrorism, while innervating for single marches, was tricky to form a long-term movement around, they moved onto the issue of child sexual exploitation by Muslims. This, however, gave anti-fascists too much space to counter them on a clear political terrain, where the DFLA had no advantages. After a march built around confusing and slightly aimless cooperation with wider pro-Brexit groups, the vitality had been drained.

Statue defenders protest

As the Black Lives Matter (BLM) protests spread to the UK in mid-2020, they caused backlash in the form of 'statue defender' protests. In Bristol, the statue of slave owner Edward Colston was toppled and dumped in the harbour. In London, a protester graffitied the Winston Churchill statue in Parliament Square with 'Churchill was a racist'. Phil Hickin, the *de facto* leader of the DFLA by virtue of running the Facebook page, responded in a reply to a comment on an unrelated post that the DFLA would be marching in response. This casualness is significant.

Nationalism, in either its 'pisshead' or (to quote Patriotic Alternative's leader) its 'winebar' variations, is politically basic – it is an almost ambient idea for many people. This ideologically basicness is not necessarily a drawback. One pleasure of fascism is its mindlessness. But it does change the relationship between the swarm and the influencers. In a previous chapter, we noted that one of the far-right influencer's functions is to declare something weaponisable. In the statue defence protests, this function of pointing at something to weaponise it was undercut. Unable to explicitly call on anti-Black racism, the far-right influencers in this case were left expressing something entirely obvious. Churchill is not a symbol that needs explaining to the far right. Even Tommy Robinson's usually assured command of the crowd's mood was redundant compared to the impetus of the crowd itself. Because he no longer needed to direct attention or articulate ideology, he amped up the emotional intensity instead, releasing a histrionic video to his remaining followers on the Russian version of Facebook, VK. The question of what role influencers might take once the politics has become obvious to everyone has not yet been resolved.

Robinson did not attend the protest. There, the crowd's mood rapidly escalated, as if their purpose on coming on the march was to fight the police and little else. Fighting the police, after all, is entertaining, and antagonism towards police might have been brewing during the preceding coronavirus lockdown. However, there is a longer history of anti-police antagonism, expressed through the resonance between the space of the march and the space of the football stadium. Both are highly directed (towards victory in football and outrage in politics) and thus intensely affective spaces – explicitly male – other forms of which were temporarily denied to everyone under lockdown (the pub most importantly). By the time of the 2020 protests, football hooliganism had become again more prominent in the DFLA; different firms had called a truce for the day. Like the question of the influencers, the future place of footballing culture in the far right remains to be resolved.

US STREET MOVEMENTS

Charlottesville

The Unite the Right Rally was a major turning point for the alt-right: what was supposed to be its gateway to real power turned out to be the beginnings of its decline. This disaster for them, largely triggered by the murder of anti-fascist Heather Heyer, is comprehensible in terms of the dynamics we have elaborated thus far: members of a fervent swarm trained in a digital environment built around their own potency and unable to apprehend the limits of their power, recklessly attacked their enemies and thus undermined the movement's reproductive capacity. This is *not* to suggest that the killer operated as a 'lone wolf'. The construction of an image of violent potency escalating into murder was a collective process. In the words of Christopher Cantwell (also known as The Crying Nazi because of his weepy appearance in a VICE documentary), the point of the march was to make the far right "more capable of violence."[64]

The consequences of the march for the alt-right were many. Most significantly, it put them more firmly into the American national consciousness. The alt-right was no longer simply a bogeyman conjured by the Democrats during the 2016 election, but a real danger. It deepened the resolve of anti-fascists and demonstrated to the wider public the necessity of opposing the far right. Metapolitically, it called a halt to their fawning presentation in the media as 'dapper' or 'hip'.

It also complexified their relationship to Trump: he famously refused to condemn them, but those who stayed within the movement in the aftermath were more likely to be sceptical of conventional political routes for their ideas, Trump included. Charlottesville caused structural changes in the wider movement. In their attempt to self-differentiate, it sheared the movement of its 'alt-lite' wing and split other organisations internally, perhaps most significantly Patriot Front, who emerged from a Discord-based palace coup inside Vanguard America. It was a smaller, much more hard-line, and much less publicly tolerated alt-right that persisted after 2017.

Given that the politics expressed online were, if anything, more extreme, why was it only when the far right entered the street that its danger was understood by mainstream culture? Internet politics and the posting of political imagery online is widely taken to be profoundly unserious. Moreover, the adoption of Pepe the Frog as the emblem of the movement, even when set alongside neo-Nazi imagery, obscured the group's radicalism. When the alt-right arrived in real space holding giant swastika flags – the same flags they had used as profile pictures for a year – they were suddenly understood. Charlottesville failed for the alt-right as much because of optics as because of murder. In its aftermath, figures such as the aforementioned 'Groyper army' of Nick Fuentes shifted tactics from developing an autonomous movement to influencing the mainstream Republican Party.

BLM and Kyle Rittenhouse

Charlottesville was only a taste of what was to come in the twilight of Trump's presidency. The original BLM uprisings in 2014 took place in a radically different context to those in 2020. The street has become less a staging point for demonstrations and more a zone of ongoing disorder in which competing forces – BLM, 'antifa', local police, federal agents, 'Boogaloo Bois', and '3 percenter' militias – vie for power. The instant circulation of images of the chaos from smartphones across social media contributes to this sense of insurrectionary potential.

The policing has also somewhat changed. Although Obama deployed the National Guard in Ferguson, there is something different in Trump's use of interagency taskforce and the rank explicitness of the comity between the police and far-right paramilitaries. 17-year-old Kyle Rittenhouse, who allegedly killed two people in sight of the police, was nonetheless allowed to go back home. Trump blamed the unrest on "left-wing political violence", claiming that, if he hadn't been armed, Rittenhouse "probably would have been killed." He cited selectively edited video of the Rittenhouse attack to portray the anti-racist activists as the aggressors – video spread by the far right. Here as elsewhere, the far right imposes a kind of *order* by conjuring the threat of serious disorder and widespread killing.

This episode brought greater clarity to the interpenetration of the state and militia movements. The state is by far the dominant force in public space. Nothing else comes close.

Nevertheless, the state cannot do everything it wants. It is curtailed (except when dealing with black people) to some extent by the law, a curtailment it pushes against unevenly. It is this constraint that allows for neo-Nazi groups to present themselves as the true form of law and order – the police having been 'cucked' by the left or 'controlled' by the conspiracy theory of the deep state. Militia groups are not so constrained and are useful to the state, even if their alliance is only implicit. However, in the case of the Boogaloo boys, their anti-state, anti-police dimension prevented, for the most part, this kind of coordination. Instead, tensions between different parts – some arguing for private property ownership as the foundational promise of America and some for racial supremacy – meant that the complexity of the group resisted easy *functionalisation* by the state in any particular form.

In the aftermath of the 2020 election, a group, as heterogeneous as those who had appeared at Charlottesville, stormed the US Capitol, attempting to prevent the ratification of the electoral college's votes for President. This movement, in distinction from that which had appeared at Charlottesville, was composed of a motley group of conspiracy theorists motivated by QAnon, rather than ideological fascists. For these groups, the powers of the state were something to be seized, and the last vestiges of its pure military power to be appealed to. Simultaneously, the COVID-19 pandemic had accelerated the normie uptake of far-right views, incorporating communities as diverse as the wellness industry and the militia movement. Cleansing of the state was the goal; cleansing of the body the means. By early 2021, far-right politics in America had attained an almost totally mythical character, divorced often from even the mainstays of far-right thinking on race or the nation conventionally understood. In response, liberals exaggerated the threat, pushing the US into a further cycle of escalating the power of its security forces.

———————

The street remains the most important test for far-right politics. The order it has historically sought to impose is unavailable to it. First, this is because of the ever-increasing dominance of the state in public space. Second, it is because the street is now bordered at every point by the internet, and the possibility of its spectacular networked representation elsewhere. And the network is only interested in images of disorder. In the next chapter, we explore the organisational forms that have emerged to lend coherence to the disparate parts of the far right we have so far discussed, and explore in particular those that, through their stunt making, have attempted to systematically produce images full of the tension between far-right order and spectacular disorder.

NEW ORGANISATIONAL FORMS

As life collided with the internet, traditional far-right parties became seemingly outmoded. The dynamism of the swarm was able to outpace its own governance, cause shock and outrage, and capture sustained mainstream attention. It made far-right parties seem old, cranky, and boring by comparison. That doesn't mean they disappeared: in some countries they still remain the dominant force on the far right. And even where they are not as dominant, their effects are still felt throughout it.

But they have transformed, and new forms of hybrid structure have appeared, combining the speed and connectivity, as well as the image-consciousness of online activism, with the organisational consistency of a party. Organisations such as Generation Identity (a pan-European group with local chapters across continental Europe) and the American Identity Movement, previously called Identity Evropa (a group which translated, at times awkwardly, Identitarianism into an American context), are the most prominent examples. Other notable examples include the UK's Patriotic Alternative, Belgium's Schild & Vrienden, and Italy's CasaPound, from whom GI borrowed the idea of a network of physical spaces.

These are the type of organisation that strive to encompass all the aspects of the modern far right that we have discussed so far: largely recruiting young men online, they operate metapolitically to propagate conspiracies such as The Great Replacement, produce reams of content as far-right influencers, operationalise the swarm (which they feed, in turn, with videos and images of their stunts), puff themselves up as the youthful action-focused wing of an intellectual tradition, and participate in street actions and stunts. However, as this chapter and the next will show, this degree of smooth integration is somewhat illusory, and contradictions remain, both internally and with the mass shooters to their right. In recent years, the prominence of these organisations, at least in Europe, has diminished slightly, as the broad base of support for non-electoral far-right politics has ebbed, and thus the social consequences of showing one's face as part of an organisation dedicated to far-right stunt-making (where the fact of being someone in particular, unafraid to show their face, is integral to the power of the images) have become clearer and more damaging.

In the absence of the sense of ascendency, this above-ground far right was unable to sustain itself for long. Activists who were once proud to show their faces went back underground or were shamed out of the movement entirely. This does not mean that these organisations are gone, only that their newer formations have become more security-conscious and anonymous. Recent forms of far-right organisation have returned to symbol-making without putting their bodies on the line – for example, the Hundred Handers network, which produces highly anonymised stickers with suggestively racist slogans for unknown activists to place in mundane locations.

Nevertheless, the particular formulation of components that new organisations use remains a potent one. The question identitarianism – a form of far-right political thinking which puts the defence of a nested hierarchy of identities at the heart of politics – seeks to answer in the affirmative is: 'Is it useful, in the age of the internet, for the far right to have long-term organisations?' It is worth us asking too.

Thinking, by analogy, about the various functions of long-term organisations in the ecosystem of the left might be a useful way to begin. There, organisations are useful for multiple reasons, one of which is their ability to sustain institutional memory, a problem of fringe movements generally. Without it, little gets passed down from moment to moment. The blooming of groups on Telegram, concerned entirely with propagating 'fashwave' images,[65] is a function of this lack of institutional memory, and its replacement with a fully mythic sense of the movement's inherent, but obscured, potency (its unrecaptureable 'meme magic'). Organisations are also infrastructural: they prevent churn, operate to persuade people to return endlessly to politics, but they also function as containers, spaces for conviviality, and provide established places for new recruits to go when there is a big influx of interest.

At their limits, totalising institutions supply their members with three basic things: total explanation (everything that happens is explicable through the group); total identity (the group clarifies who you are, and membership is the central marker of that identity); and total activity (you have always a clear sense of what to do).

Of course, organisational structure can also be a hindrance to politics: the alt-right, probably the most successful far-right movement of recent times, lacked substantial organisational form. One problem that the US far right faced for a long time before the 'swarm' became a viable organisational form itself was that their organisations (Aryan Nations, National Alliance, and so on) were so self-evidently terrible that, when there was a big surge in numbers, it simply increased the size of the existing organisations or formed organisations like them and repeated their mistakes.

IDENTITARIANISM

Identitarianism takes its cues from the European New Right. It claims that racial and cultural identity are at the root of politics, but that these identities are complex, and exist at multiple scales. Less concerned with the nation state than nationalists (and therefore, often more so with race), identitarians have attempted to build a pan-European network of activists who will defend 'White culture' or 'European civilisation' more broadly. The most prominent of these groups, Generation Identity, has spread across Europe from their beginnings in France and Austria and, via the UK, had been attempting to crack America, which failed in part because of the stubbornness of existing British nationalist culture. In March 2021, they were banned in France. They have cloaked their racism in jargon and positioned themselves as non-violent, but their politics point towards genocide. Of all the groups discussed in this book, Generation Identity is arguably the one most able to integrate all the different aspects of a contemporary far-right group.

These groups, despite appearing very much at home on the internet, were formed before social media. The street movement Jeunesses Identitaires (JI) – 'young identitarians' – was formed in 2002, followed by Bloc Identitaire (BI) in 2003, which provided the emerging identitarian network with support. JI was replaced by Une Autre Jeunesse ('another youth') and then Génération Identitaire (GI) in 2012. Whilst Les Identitaires and GI are independent, they publicly support one another.

Generation Identity's status as a youth movement is important. Their English-language website and manifestos declare 'war on the baby boomers' – those who have grown fat on the surpluses of the last few decades. This generational aggression is both tactically and strategically effective: both because it allows a more general cult of youth to emerge, and also because different generations are positioned extremely differently with regards to the problems of society at the largest scale (migration, declining workplace power, the saturation of culture with the internet and, not least, climate change). They have recruited mostly at universities. More broadly, the cult of youth is a specific articulation of the idea of the 'last man', and the utility of the stunts these groups carry out is in demonstrating masculine potency as much as in performing specific actions. This kind of populist generational conflict (a description of conflict that obscures the contributions of baby boomers to political struggle and the deep distinctions within them as a generation wherever it is deployed) also, in this case, obscures the institutional intertwining of Generation Identity's politics with the *status quo*. Generation Identity, despite its cult of youth, shares with other recent organisations the position of being the *de facto* youth wing of a larger far-right grouping and the far right is, whatever its revolutionary pretentions, more often than not simply the more explicit and militant wing of the forces of social discipline.

The success of the groups across Europe has been highly uneven: while it was treated in 2018, at least in the UK, as the principal far-right threat of the moment, after successful groups had launched in Germany, Austria, and France, by early 2020 this UK chapter had farcically imploded and its importance as the new standard in far-right organising in

Europe had waned. What led to this assessment, and what led to this decline?

The assessment was led first of all by the comparative slickness of their presentation. The actions of Generation Identity are often spectacular and their graphic design impressive. Their YouTube videos are edited to more or less the going standard, their leaders are presentable and articulate, their colour scheming and branding is tight, their stunts are simple but sharp, and they reject symbols that would tie them too easily to the fascist past. This symbolic discipline allows GI to work particularly effectively in places where explicit neo-Nazi ideology is banned.

But this is to give them far too much credit. Aesthetic slickness masked a deep organisational insufficiency and a great deal of incompetence. In mid-2019, the UK branch of Generation Identity was expelled from the European organisation for allowing a well-known antisemite to speak at their conference. That same event was also infiltrated by an undercover reporter, who GI had given the task of photographing the event. Hardly the work of a flawless organisation, and perhaps a lesson against the transformation more generally of politics into branding.

It is nevertheless undeniable that in the wider-European context, GI has produced some impressive looking stunts. Stunts appeal to an urge for vitality: they demonstrate commitment in an age of uncommitted politics. GI's stunt atop the Brandenburg Gate with the banner (in German) "safe borders – safe future" attempts to transform this staid but still multifaceted monument back into a living symbol of something they seek to recover. While the Gate is today a pacified tourist attraction serving as a generic symbol of post-reunification Germany and sometimes the EU more generally, the choice of attraction is obviously made to invoke a mythic past, more glorious and daring than the present.

However, the spectacular quality of much of Generation Identity's activism should not be confused with fluffiness or unaggressive media campaigning. Other stunts appeal to the straightforwardly violent pole of the state. Interwar fascist groups imposed order on cities where, they asserted, the state had failed to. In contemporary statecraft, the police no longer wage battles in the city with throngs of communists, at least in Europe. Instead, the point of maximum influence over the state, from its paramilitary outside, has become the border. This is where the state is most obviously murderous, but the details are obscured by its distance from the metropolitan heartland, and emotionally blunted by racism. It is here that Generation Identity's most famous and arguably most two important stunts attempted to intervene.

The 2017 Defend Europa campaign involved the mobilisation of a global far-right network to fund a boat in the Mediterranean to 'police' the crossing of migrants into Europe. The stunt was a metapolitical success. On the ground, the boat was beset by problems, unable to dock in Sicily due to anti-racist protests and needing to be rescued after running into difficulties. Defend Europa, like the later alpine crossing stunt, was designed to be seen rather than be effective.

Is the Defend Europa campaign an example of contemporary paramilitarism? Not quite. Mostly it consisted in goading the state through propaganda into fulfilling the state's own functions in ways that satisfied the far right. In this way the conservatism of the actions, and not fascism, is revealed. All that is asked of the state is that it fulfil its legal obligations. Framed like this, identitarianism looks a lot more like a pressure group – a kind of youth version of the TaxPayers' Alliance[66] – and much of the revolutionary aesthetics drop away.

What the state conceals, GI attempts to make visceral. The purpose is to make suffering spectacular, a logic that also explains the popular, transparent sadism of much of the Trump administration's border policies. Martin Sellner explains the action as essentially journalistic: they are attempting to produce, he says, an 'image of corruption' – the point at which the profound wrongness of contemporary border policing becomes evident to the supposed audience. They imagine a revelatory moment at which what is obvious to them becomes obvious to everyone. However, like much of far-right metapolitics, this only works if you have already entered their mindset. GI, the normie-revolutionaries, imagine both that they are more radical than they are and that their ideas are more widely shared. Identitarianism presents itself as a revolutionary project, but in truth at its heart is nothing but the tedium of the status quo.

We can see a similar kind of continuity between previous far-right movements and the disciplinary apparatus of the state.

The far-right counter-Jihad movement acted as the more explicitly political wing of the state's anti-Muslim policing in the aftermath of 9/11. They require each other: the state requires the far right to support electorally its expansion of control over heavily policed communities, and the far right needs the state as a foil for its anger and campaigns.

In the Defend Europa campaign, as well, we can see the contiguity of the whole right. In early 2020, Greek fascists shot at migrants on boats in the Aegean Sea. Arguably, the action is modelled on the Defend Europa stunt. The slogan for the Defend Europa – "No Way, You Will Not Make Europe Home" – was copied from an anti-migration campaign designed in 2016 by Scott Morrison, who later became the Australian Prime Minister. This is how the right feeds the far right, and the far right feeds murder.

GI has also appeared regularly at street demonstrations. In Europe, where they are more powerful, they have made their own street movements, and adopted a style somewhere between classical fascism and the Kendall Jenner Pespi ad. In the UK, they appeared sporadically at street demonstrations organised by more prominent far-right influencers, and used the larger mass as cover to recruit and have a presence without worrying about disruption from anti-fascists.

WHAT IS THE SIGNIFICANCE OF IDENTITARIANISM?

The significance of identitarianism lies in its openness to other forms of far-right thinking and its disregard of the usually sacrosanct norms of national far rights. Into an identitarian frame can slip more or less any concern: reactionary gender politics, environmentalism, immigration, the issues of cultural identity, anti-Muslim racism, or local beautification projects. This is because identitarianism is less a specific project than a frame for engaging with politics as a whole. As long as a concern can be understood as an expression of culture (which is more or less anything once you have declared science to be 'essentially white') it is of relevance to identitarianism. But we should not place identitarianism strictly into a cultural register. Its concerns are not those of British ruralists writing in the early 20th century on the joys of Morris dancing. Rather, identitarians organise for transparently political outcomes, for example the mass deportation of non-white populations (what they term 'remigration').

Although Alain de Benoist, in his *Manifesto for a European Renaissance*, bemoans the excessive utility of the internet, and the spread of technological values of operability, efficiency and performance, to some extent identitarianism is a political formation specific to the age of the internet. At the very least, the suspension of tensions between national far-right cultures has allowed identitarianism to form itself into a separate mode of politics. It matters a lot if the French new right and the German right are talking online or if they are having separate national conversations. And the grounds for this possibility are not only Anglophone culture but, perversely, the integrationist logic of the European Union.

The internet has also contributed to an internationalisation of the identitarian movement – a process in which uneven local far-right cultures are reorganised, with varying degrees of success, by identitarians. Incidents, images, videos or narratives particular to a local context are echoed around the identitarian world and woven into an interconnected metanarrative. The internet, which is both the site of spectacular action and of deep conventional sluggishness (understood by the far right as the degeneracy of the Nietzschean 'last man') not only makes the acceleration of metapolitics possible, but makes *acceleration itself* the main metapolitical content to be transmitted. 'We can go faster, life can be more thrilling' is the message of the stunts. But this acceleration, too, has blandly racist pan-Europeanist content when it becomes concrete.

Although it is not the political vehicle of their choosing, enthusiasm for the European Union amongst German and Austrian youth might account for something of the ease in which a civilizational as opposed to a national racism is expressed in the far right. Lower levels of enthusiasm, and even overwhelming scepticism, amongst older generations of the far right in the UK, might go some way to explaining the comparative floundering of identitarianism in Britain. Still, for identitarianism more generally, the state is not the important object of politics, as it was in past generations, but is simply the available expression of a fundamental national function, which could be achieved through any number of other means, including the EU. If, as has often been claimed, the far right thrive on contradictions that exist within capitalism, then perhaps the uninteresting answer about identitarianism is that it thrives off the contradictions between the humanitarian European self-image as encapsulated in the EU and the persistent inability of that union to instantiate its values.

In the American context, identitarianism has been less prominent, perhaps because 'whiteness' rather than specific national identity has often been the basis for the American far right's politics. Identity Evropa, later renamed American Identity Movement (AIM), was founded in 2016 by Nathan Damigo, an Iraq War veteran (a connection particularly significant in the US, where Vietnam veterans also formed much of the White Power movement in the 70s and 80s).[67] AIM placed its propaganda in libraries and explicitly thought of itself as taking the tools of the left: Saul Alinsky is a seemingly unlikely touchpoint. Like Generation Identity, universities were their main target, where they have explicitly understood themselves as "taking up space", a phrase from the left-wing protest handbook. In 2020, on the eve of the US election, they disbanded.

PATRIOTIC ALTERNATIVE

In 2019, the collapse of the Identitarian Movement (formerly Generation Identity UK) and the slow decline of the civic nationalist movements surrounding Tommy Robinson and UKIP presented an opening on the British far right, which at the time of writing has been taken up by a new organisation – Patriotic Alternative (PA). What should interest us here is not PA as a political entity *per se* but the organisational form they are attempting to pioneer – one that has viability beyond a particular group.

At present, PA is still a marginal force. In 2019 and 2020, they organised three moderate-sized conferences, a smattering of camping trips, a national survey project and a series of 'White Lives Matter' banner drops to coincide with Indigenious People's Day. In many ways, the party is a deliberate throwback to the British National Party (BNP). Its leader, Mark Collett, held prominent positions within the BNP. The BNP was, of course, the most successful fascist party in Britain since the Second World War.

PA have borrowed significant political positions from the BNP, namely a focus on the preservation of a white Britain through a promotion of traditional family values, voluntary repatriation schemes (as with other identitarians, this is a seemingly mild proposition whose logical end point is ethnic cleansing), an inverted theory of racism that sees whites as the oppressed group within Britain, and a barely veiled anti-semitism. PA's appropriation of indigeneity discourses is also taken directly from the BNP. PA have followed the BNP in their tactics, eschewing street demonstrations and instead launching smaller actions like the 'We Were Never Asked' project, which purported to be a survey of attitudes about immigration.

However, the two are not identical. Unlike the BNP, which split from the National Front and thus started with a base of experienced activists, PA do not have a ready base of activists from which to draw, largely because of the decade-long gap since the collapse of the BNP. Their initial base is an integration of the audiences of a network of ethnonationalist content creators. So far, internal community building has taken precedence over external activism.

Recruitment from these audiences has both advantages and drawbacks. Consumption of ethnonationalist content has a low threshold of participation and doesn't attract much risk. In comparison to the laborious and public process of joining the BNP, these days you don't even have to leave your bedroom to get into ethnonationalism. Much as with the alt-right, the process of radicalisation can take place away from the eyes of loved ones, the authorities, or anti-fascists. The entrainment that consuming such content produces happens here in more stable communities than it did in the alt-right, often in group chats where a small number of ever-present superusers stand ready to call out unwanted behaviour, especially the endlessly possible turn to 'blackpilled' pessimism. These superusers also mask a complicated split in the group over the possible efficacy of the democratic path for ethnonationalism.

Poaching creators associated with Tommy Robinson and the civic nationalist side of the far right has been a major plank of PA's strategy. This process is going on at the level of individuals: though Mark Collett has positioned himself against the 'ego-led' street movements of the 'Tommy gang', his technique nevertheless relies on the conversion and mobilisation of those same personalities.

A reliance on audiences for an activist base does create problems. One of the major issues for PA is the problem of turning an anonymous mass of content consumers and shitposters into committed and therefore also identifiable activists without making them more vulnerable. PA have tried to work around this by keeping their IRL actions relatively closed and making efforts to hide the identities of most participants, even when they are acting in the real world among trusted fellow activists. As PA attracts more attention, and more sustained opposition from anti-fascists, their ability to engage in public activities anonymously will be further and further reduced.

PA, in the UK context, has some advantages over GI. To their detriment, Generation Identity UK was forced to abide by the sensibilities of the major continental groups, which did not suit a British context. Pan-Europeanism is a hard sell in a scene so heavily invested in Brexit and the inclusion of 'Éire' in the branch name also did not sit well, given the long history of anti-Irish racism on the British far right. PA are also not weighed down by the same carefulness around anti-semitism, an issue that ultimately saw GI expelled from the identitarian movement.

There has always been a divide in the British far right between civic nationalists, who do not believe an individual has to belong to a particular race to belong to a nation, and ethnonationalists, who subscribe to a biological racist view that believes that only those of a particular race can belong to a nation. PA have placed themselves firmly on the ethnonationalist side of the debate and have played an active role in swinging the British far right towards ethnonationalism. For the time being, however, the existence of a substantial civic nationalist movement in the UK forms their main chance to grow. Not being sufficiently large to overcome anti-fascist disruption, PA need to appeal mostly to those already in the movement, who they can radicalise further. For now, PA seems to require a broader, civic nationalist far right, to even exist.

WHAT NEXT?

These new organisational forms have the capacity, or at least aspire, to tie together all different forms of far-right organising. Recently, however, as the wider cultural milieu surrounding the far right has waned online, identitarian groups have begun to fade from the limelight. Such a transition can make people tend toward despair. There has been a long-running tension on the fascist and neo-Nazi far right between those who wish to emphasise the positive and life-affirming discourse of fascism and those who are committed to its violent tactics. Within groups like Patriotic Alternative there are constant battles being waged by influencers to stem the tendency towards blackpilling and promote a hopeful 'white pill' in which its members are engaged in productive, helpful activities. Blackpilling – the belief that there is no political solution and therefore extreme violence is justified – seems to nevertheless happen anyway.

Generation Identity has clearly been damaged by the news that the Christchurch shooter donated money to the Austrian branch of the movement and exchanged emails with its *de facto* leader, Martin Sellner. This was not only because the links drew investigation from the Austrian state but also because their flagship conspiracy theory, The Great Replacement, was the title of the shooter's manifesto.

Their connections with the terrorists to their right, as well as their rapidly declining claims to something like counter-cultural insurgency, has blunted their potency, at least for now. Martin Sellner's new project *Die Osterreicher* ('The Austrians') has abandoned the pan-Europeanist politics and youth orientation of GI for a more conventional patriotic anti-immigration politics, dropping for now the stunts by which he made his name. This, along with specific anti-fascist targeting and complicated legal troubles, has led to the decline of the identitiarian movement.

The main trick of these new organisational forms, particularly identitarians, was to specifically *not* appear as Nazis, who are clearly still disliked by the public at large. But for all their claims to innovation, these movements still haven't found a way to escape this historical context. Leaders and activists have histories very much rooted in more obviously neo-Nazi politics and, as we have seen, the new movements are still set within the wider far right. Whether allied or in conflict with other parts of the far right, new organisational forms are still associated with them. In the context of impending climate breakdown, the far right's best hope still lies in these new organisational innovations, especially if sufficient firewalls can be developed to allow the more straightforwardly murderous aspects of the far right to complement rather than damage movements. It may take a whole new paradigm – that of ecofascism – for them to succeed. We will discuss both these deadly aspects and the possibilities of ecofascism in the final two chapters of this book.

DEADLY VIOLENCE

––––––––––

Deadly violence is nothing new on the far right. Violence played a key function in the rise of fascist states. Fascism had to be *seen* to be capable of wielding violence. From the 1910s, paramilitary organisations enforced the will of fascist leaders. But, at least in some periods, this capacity for wielding violence has had to be curtailed lest it alienate more passive supporters. In January 1925, Mussolini made a speech to the Chamber of Deputies: he claimed responsibility for the violence of his blackshirts and challenged his opponents to remove him. He then took charge of restoring order to Italy within forty-eight hours. This tension between order and violence – order *as* violence and the command of chaos – lasts until this day.

Violence doesn't happen randomly or from nowhere. Nor do far-right terrorists murder from personal conviction alone. Both extreme ideology and a structure of radicalisation are required. Even the incomparable darkness of the Holocaust can be understood as arising from a combination of extreme ideology and a collection of mechanisms of radicalisation, both internal and external to Nazism.[68] Ideology provides the tracks along which the motor of radicalisation pushes people towards deadly violence.

INDIVIDUALS AND GROUPS

After WWII political violence is taboo, even if ubiquitous – non-state groups that are seen to support it face sanction from the increasingly powerful state. Regardless, some far-right groups have explicitly supported deadly violence. Since the much-mythologised Manson Family and the explicitly neo-Nazi National Socialist Liberation Front (NSLF), there has been a terroristic wing to Anglophone post-war far-right groups. In the 1980s, The Order – taking its cues from William Pierce's *The Turner Diaries* (on which more to come) – murdered radio show host Alan Berg.

However, these groups have largely been small and ineffective – indeed, smallness and ineffectiveness themselves breed frustration that explodes into violence. One of the main concerns of far-right groups seeking continuity has thus been to curtail their more radical members. Both Joseph Tomassi and George Lincoln Rockwell (the founders of the NSLF and the American Nazi Party, respectively) failed: they were killed by their own disgruntled subordinates and rivals. It was in the early 1980s, with the innovation of 'leaderless resistance' in the US militia movement, dispersing the wider movement into cell-type structures to prevent its decapitation, that the first half-successful exculpation of the wider movement from the actions of its radical edge occurred.

It was not entirely effective. In 1995, the Oklahoma City Bombing was carried out by Timothy McVeigh and Terry Nichols, killing 168 people (like other attacks, such as those by The Order, it was based on the opening attack of *The Turner Diaries*). The wider militia and White Power movements – the latter ascendant since the return of veterans from the Vietnam war – were severely damaged by the bombing. It ended one period of deadly violence in the US. In 1999, David Copeland (ex-BNP and National Socialist Movement member) bombed LGBT, Black, and Bengali communities in London, killing three people, effectively ending the period of violence dominated by groups like Combat-18 in the UK. He, too, was inspired by *The Turner Diaries*.

Anders Breivik

If one wave of far-right terrorism ended in the late 90s, as its effects on the wider far right discouraged it, another was to begin as the counter-jihad movement gained strength and coherence in the early 2010s. Nevertheless, Anders Breivik, who killed 77 people in Norway in 2011, many of them children, was not connected to organised far-right groups. His radicalisation was stimulated by the blogs of the counter-jihad movement, a connection tenuous enough for them to escape substantial blowback from his actions. While Breivik recognised the need for widespread circulation of his ideas, and the capacity for the internet to help in this, he did not become radicalised initially (a process he dates to 2002) in an online *community*. His status as the first far-right mass shooter of the social media age is thus complicated.

Dylann Roof

In 2015, Dylann Roof entered a Black church in South Carolina and murdered nine attendees of a bible study group. His radicalisation also did not take place through organised white nationalist communities online. Instead, he radicalised through propaganda published by the Council of Conservative Citizens – a white nationalist group that cloaks its politics in the garb of conservatism but which refused to disavow his actions entirely. Roof did not circulate a manifesto before his attack; afterwards it was discovered that he had registered a website, lastrhodesian. com, on which he hosted an unsigned manifesto that offered an explanation for his attack as well as laying out his views on race in more detail. His connections with the organised far right were tenuous before he committed his murders; however, his distinctive bowl cut allowed for the far right to develop a way of jokingly discussing murder. 'Taking the bowl pill' (a reference to the redpill meme) and the phrase 'take me to church' became code for committing acts of violence. His actions were recycled into the far-right meme canon and became part of the common language of violence.

The total number of incidents of far-right terrorism has more than trebled in the past five years. This rise in absolute numbers comes with several other changes: in the last decade, right-wing political motivations have been attached to a third of mass shootings in the US, up from one in five over the three decades before that. These attacks are rarely organised by groups. Instead, almost all are organised and prosecuted by 'lone wolf' individuals. Perpetrators rarely have physical contact with others on the far right. The men who plan and carry out these attacks rarely have "definite in-person contact with other far-right individuals or groups, and over a third appear to have been primarily radicalised online." Indeed, "in the US in 2018, there were no recorded attacks at all by a known terrorist group."[69]

What does this change mean for the categorisation of violence? We might begin by suggesting that there are three types of deadly violence on the far right: squad violence, scripted violence, and stochastic terrorism. 'Squad violence' is the principle output of a particular kind of 'blackpilled' group, such as Atomwaffen in the US, the National Socialist Underground in Germany, or National Action in the UK. 'Scripted violence' is modelled on the pronouncements of influencers or groups, which do not explicitly call for attacks but where violence is an implied solution or natural outcome. It is carried out by people separated from those organisations or influencers, often by some distance, which allows them to deny responsibility. 'Stochastic terrorism' is at an even further remove: it is not the fulfilment of a nameable group's intentions but the product of a febrile, violent mood produced in communities. Indeed, it may be difficult to establish any link to the organised far right at all.

These categories are not as distinct as they might initially seem. The difference between 'scripted violence' and 'stochastic terrorism' is perhaps only one of degree, and in the aftermath of an attack it is not uncommon for connections to slowly come to light. Indeed, the idea of a far-right terrorist entirely isolated from the organisations of the far right might simply be a fantasy of a naive 'bad apple' model of terrorism. Were the Christchurch Mosque attacks 'scripted violence'? The shooter's manifesto was named, after all, after a conspiracy theory propagated by Generation Identity. Or were they 'stochastic terrorism', because the shooter was not involved with the group except through donating money? Or were they 'squad violence', because he had been radicalised in a community online?

Why make and then break such distinctions? Assigning causality to an action is necessarily fraught in general. In the contemporary far right, where navigation between its parts is so fluid and membership no longer a clearly defined status, it becomes almost impossible. Deadly violence, instead, is one kind of 'ecological output' of the entirety of the far right – a generality that doesn't prevent precise and directed action from being taken against it.

Until the internet, 'radicalisation structures' largely meant named, organised groups who had external recruitment and internal education processes to turn non-fascists into fascists. Groups, moreover, have different wings: often a split between moderates and radicals. Crucially, these groups' own continuity is threatened by the actions of a radical wing, so there is an incentive to moderate their more extreme members. For radicalisation to take place and for this to coexist supportively with existing far-right organisations, there thus needed to be a radicalisation mechanism not tied to the group form. This is what the swarm provides.

This radicalisation has at least two broad themes: the construction of an ideological justification, and the process of collective confirmation of this ideology. This takes place, even if the perpetrator of the deadly violence never actually has in-person contact. First, we will discuss the ideology.

EXTREME IDEOLOGY

In distinction to the violence of fascist parties in the pre-war period, and from the fascist violence within the Second World War (which was of a different order entirely), the violence in the period since the late 1960s does not aim to establish a particular political order or to achieve political goals as they are conventionally understood. Instead, as we will show, violence gradually became the end in itself.

The Turner Diaries

In 1978, William Luther Pierce – leader of the neo-Nazi group National Alliance – wrote *The Turner Diaries*. Told through the eyes of protagonist Earl Turner, the novel depicts the ultimately successful struggle of a white supremacist group called The Organization, which carries out dizzyingly graphic acts of violence, ultimately culminating in nuclear Armageddon. The novel has acted, for neo-Nazis, as a predictor of events to come, a blueprint for action, and a tool of political education. Like Harold Covington's *The Brigade* and William Lind's *Victoria: A Novel of 4th Generation War*, the novel provides both the problem – a shadowy world government controlled by Jews that attacks whites – and the solution – fascist terror and, ultimately, global race war.

The Turner Diaries strips fascist ideology of its particularity. The political persuasion of The Organization (the novel's protagonist terroristic organisation) is not explained during the narrative beyond a basic framework of white supremacy, the need for violence and an 'anti-System' revolutionism. This making-generic of ideology was taken further by David Lane, a member of the aforementioned group The Order, who boiled this ideology down to just 14 words, "We must secure the existence of our people and a future for white children," a mantra still referenced by white supremacists today. It supplies the '14' in the phrase '14/88'. The '88' is for 'Heil Hitler'.

SIEGE

There are, nevertheless, still terrorist groups. Online, first the website Iron March and later Fascist Forge served as both forum and recruiting ground for new groups, most famously the American neo-Nazi group Atomwaffen. For Atomwaffen, it was the revival of a past generation's writings – particularly those of an ex-member of the NSLF, James Mason – that was most influential in the revival and spread of 'blackpilled' fascism, permissive of acts of cataclysmic violence. *SIEGE*, written by Mason over the course of six years in the 80s, was a newsletter describing the necessity of an all-out assault on the nebulous 'System'. It gloried in violence. Users of Iron March tracked down Mason, then living in obscurity, and convinced him to start writing again. It is down to the obsessions of online fascist nerds that *SIEGE* has had any influence on the far right today. In his writings, violence becomes something of an end in itself.

Islam and the O9A

A manic absolutism about violence as an end in itself has another source: the significantly better-known and more broadly feared violence of Salafi-Jihadism. Salafi-Jihadism is looked at as a serious and committed form of reactionary politics that contains a similar cult of violence and death. One member of Atomwaffen killed two others after they mocked his conversion to Islam. Stripped of the belief in an afterlife, the violence of neo-Nazi groups takes inspiration from them, but removes the possibility of divine redemption, excepting the worship of the living. Online, spree shooters are canonised as saints. While an account of reciprocal radicalisation (in which groups and individuals on the far right and Jihadist terrorists radicalise each other through escalating violence) might hold for some parts of the far right,[70] increasingly the influence of Islam on 'blackpilled' groups leads to *convergent radicalisation*.

Other groups, which may or may not be real, have also contributed to this ideology of violence. For example, Satanist neo-Nazi group Order of Nine Angles (O9A), advocate the killing of 'mundanes' as part process of initiation into a secretive order that ultimately enables access to the 'acausal realm'. Theirs is a prime example of the making-generic of ideology, the transformation of political struggle into a mystical one, and one of the principal sources of inter-group mistrust that endlessly befuddles blackpilled groups. In O9A materials, neo-Nazism is a mask participants must wear to self-isolate from society in pursuit of Satanist aims, but it is just as plausible to suggest that the two ideologies are, at root, compatible. It scarcely matters. The hyper-syncretism of the 'blackpilled' right blends Satanism, Salafi-Jihadist Islam, and neo-Nazism into a complicated and heady mixture that fixates on violence while dispensing with specific justifications. Like everything else here, trolling is used as a cover, but it is also an accelerant.

VIOLENCE ITSELF

———

We might say that the ultimate aim of violence is violence itself. It is at this point when the ends of politics (what you are ultimately trying to achieve) are entirely replaced by the means (what you do to get there). We propose to understand the push towards the right as a transformation of the relation of means and ends. The further right one goes, the more means are focused on at the expense of ends. Violence itself becomes the goal, the crowning achievement.

One possible explanation of antisemitism is that the Jews are blamed for the divisions in the white community as such. The fact that white people (who the far right imagines as a single coherent group) actually seem to disagree about almost everything points to them having been tricked or duped into this disagreement. The source of this disagreement is imagined to be the Jews. Here, Jews are blamed for the very existence of politics. To the blackpilled right, nothing looks more like 'politics' than attempts to justify what one wants to do without rationale, to challenge the sovereign right to violence of every fascist partisan. This attack on politics thus manifests itself on the blackpilled right as a refusal to explain or intellectualise about politics or violence. The most fascistic element of an engagement with politics thus becomes the absolute primacy of competitive violence. Contrary to the parts of the far right discussed in our chapter on intellectuals, on the blackpilled right it is the refusal to explain one's attraction to violence – to have no need of an explanation – that characterises the elite.

Nevertheless, violence sometimes has a strategic orientation, towards 'race war'. The theory of escalating to race war adopted by the blackpilled operates similarly to a strategy of tension, or the strategy of sowing ethnic divisions adopted by Al-Qaeda in Iraq. In Charles Manson's 'Helter Skelter' scenario and Pierce's *The Turner Diaries,* the escalation of tensions between black and white people is imagined to be triggered through racialised sexual violence. The ensuing race war is not oriented towards victory but towards its own continuation. Even a book like *The Turner Diaries*, which gives a vision of a future white society, ends with denial of food to those white people who are deemed genetically inferior, despite their whiteness. The culling never stops: violence is the aim, even, or especially, when it is wrapped up in a mystical future. 'Race war' is an attempt to produce the conditions in which the martial life *per se* can be realised. What is this martial life? It is oriented towards the mass, but oppositionally. As noted in the chapter on feelings, the smaller groups become, the more they oppose themselves to the wider population. These people experience themselves as would-be warriors for a society that instead despises them. To find their place, they must make society accept a general intensification of war.

Violence, even this apparently unexplained violence, has a history. Aimé Césaire suggested fascism was colonialism-come-home.[71] This continues most obviously in the US in the widespread recruitment of far-right actors from returning veterans. In a wider historical arc, in the case of the US, where the colony existed in the same space as the nation that profited off it, little distinction was made between different forms of colonial policing: the KKK, slave patrols (which continued despite Reconstruction) and the police. The interpenetration of the contemporary far-right militia movement with the police in the US is a grim echo of this indistinction born of violence. This violence is the preservative for an existing relationship of domination. Even in its mystical abstractions, the violence of groups like Atomwaffen is connected inextricably to the mundane brutality of this violent social function.

THE EXTREMIFICATION PROCESS

We can talk of an individual's radicalisation and the swarm's 'extremification'. Even though, in any given community, participation in the swarm is transitory for most individual members, communities as a whole produce norms and standards that are collectively enforced. And, as they radicalise, they form more and more formally structured groups. How do these groups – formally structured or not – become more radicalised as a whole, and produce the collective conditions in which their individual members kill?

How this happens online is, in part, a story of the history of platforms. How the boorish obscenities of SomethingAwful became the racist edgelording of 4chan, became the neo-Nazi shitposting of 8chan, became the violence-obsessed nihilism of public Telegram channels and private Discord servers, became the distributed untraceable planning of violence on Wire, became actual killing worldwide, is answerable in part through two processes: hijacking and evolutionary bottlenecking.

There is a widespread desire to play with the edges of acceptability. Edgy spaces become popular, because edginess is fun and panders to a vengeful sense of inferiority. In the dark forest of the contemporary internet, the distribution of extreme content, even for people with conventional – or no – political views, is a short path to generating attention. Thus, hijacking conventional platforms for the display of extremism can not only popularise this content but also be profitable for platform owners. However, the rising scrutiny that mass participation in edge cultures brings pushes the owners of the platform to restrict certain kinds of discourse. Extremists are sanctioned and banned, but in the time-gap between the beginning of the hijacking and this, they can lure some people to their fallback platform. The movement grows.

This process of banning need not come from the web admins themselves: in the case of 8chan, taken offline in the aftermath of the El Paso shooting, it was CloudFlare's withdrawal of protection for the site that ultimately terminated it. Indeed, the infrastructural complexity of platforms makes them vulnerable.

Although the internet affords switching between platforms when necessary, the habits of internet use on all scales are remarkably entrenched. The extremification process takes advantage of both: hijacking of already widely-used platforms by extremist ideas takes advantage of platform inertia, and the ability to leave a platform when it cracks down on you takes advantage of the mobility.

How do these newly enlarged, more extreme groups, when pushed to another platform, change? Evolutionary bottlenecking is a process that reduces the population of a given organism, for whatever reason. If this process does (and it often does) kill the weak members of a population first, those who survive are more likely to be stronger. It is from this smaller – but, importantly, genetically less diverse – population of organisms that the next generation will regrow. In the same way, the shift from platform to platform allows for the filtering of the less committed. So, the subsequent regrowth of the movement starts from a more extreme basis.

At the end of this process lie the most extreme platforms, to which the new influx of recruits is a boon. For example, the neo-Nazi forum Iron March started relatively extreme, but it took an injection of new recruits, moved along by this extremification process, for it to escalate to committing actual violence. While any savvy internet user knew about 4chan, and perhaps 8chan, Iron March's existence was unknown to almost everyone apart from fascists themselves. As it gathered new recruits it became even more extreme, as a consequence of its own internal processes. This they described as 'purity spiralling', a process in which 'pure' views (i.e. extreme and devoid of nuance) are encouraged, resulting in an ever-intensifying extremity of expression, thought, and ultimately deadly violence.

This extremification process, while producing the conditions for terrorism, also saps the capacities of groups. More radical communities have to spend significant time decamping from dead websites or platforms that have banned them and finding the infrastructure that will agree to host them. 8chan was rehosted, very briefly, by a Russia-based web host mostly known for distributing crimeware.[72] However, they too caved under pressure, and the site again went dark. It has since reappeared, but as a shadow of its former self, where collective mistrust has become ubiquitous. Indeed, some have gone so far as to suggest that the new site is actually run by law enforcement. We will return later to this ever-present suspicion.

Another channel for communities that have been uprooted is to use more fractured social media networks that lack public-facing 'town squares', such as Telegram or Discord. However, these clearly lack much of the appeal of imageboards, and they too have been cracking down on the extreme end of the far right. The Telegram channel supposed to replace 8chan had a mere 800 members in March 2020, down from the estimated 3 million monthly visits the website was attracting in August 2019, some six months after the Christchurch shooting. However, as we will now see, there is plenty of scope for people to commit violence who have routinely visited a site no more radical than YouTube, as was the case for the Christchurch shooter.

STOCHASTIC TERRORISM

The Christchurch shooter

On the 15th March, 2019, a 28-year-old Australian man – here, 'the shooter' – killed 51 people and injured 40 more at the Al Noor Mosque and the Linwood Islamic Centre in Christchurch, New Zealand.[73] He was apprehended on his way to a third location.

He livestreamed his attack on Facebook. The video was taken down after 17 minutes, by which time it had been downloaded and mirrored extensively on other sites. The video itself, as well as stills from it, were endlessly recapitulated on 8chan, overlaid with the score-counting graphics of video games, which ticked up with every murder. Images of the shooter were photoshopped into images of a saint. If the appearance of memes after the shooting seems predictable, less so was their appearance in the manifesto itself, where the attacker jokingly claimed his radicalisation was at the hands of Candace Owens, a right-wing black woman. The jokes and memes also went beyond the manifesto: the shooter told his viewers to 'subscribe to Pewdiepie' before opening fire. Like the 'navy seal' meme, also reproduced in the manifesto, this was a popular phrase at the time. He also referenced jokes that are more obviously far right, such as the Serbian anti-Muslim nationalist song 'Remove Kebab'. Here, we see the contribution of violence to meme culture – which had been accidental in the case of Dylann Roof – becoming deliberate. Paraphrasing Hannah Arendt, we might say that these far-right shooters want access to memes even at the price of destruction.[74]

It was with the Christchurch shooting that 8chan was first used to circulate a mass shooter's manifesto. 8chan presented an ideal platform for perpetrators of mass violence to amplify their message. The absence of proactive moderation on the site, indeed the indulgence of extremity, and the concentration of relatively tech-savvy ideologically blackpilled fascists in 8chan's user base meant shooters could use the site to circumvent the usual news gatekeepers and make their manifestos go viral.

The manifesto, despite its invocation of memes, was entirely serious in other ways. Like Breivik's manifesto had been, the Christchurch shooter's manifesto was fragmented and almost unreadable except by its intended recipients on 8chan. But there is also a more coherent and developed politics at work. It was named after a conspiracy – 'the Great Replacement' – promulgated by Generation Identity. He also declared himself an 'ecofascist'.

The El Paso shooter

The manifesto released by the El Paso shooter, who killed 23 people six months later, referenced the Christchurch shooter, as he in turn had referenced Breivik. What's most astonishing about this manifesto is the lacklustre quality of the preparation, the self-admittedly 'meh' manifesto, and the lack of ideological justification. Between the fairly measured critique of immigration policy – it has the tone of a somewhat unengaged high school paper – and the act of shooting people of colour randomly in a Walmart lies a gulf of justification. "There is an abyss," Hannah Arendt wrote, "between men of brilliant and facile conceptions and men of brutal deeds and active bestiality, which no intellectual explanation is able to bridge."[75] Although fascist violence is timely and has a function in the wider fascist movement, the arguments for violence frequently don't seem to stack up. And yet it persists.

The appearance and then disappearance of a viable fascist future played a role in the timing of these shootings. Ascendancy gave confidence; then, once many people were radicalised, the coming sense of a downturn produced a need to act decisively while there was still time. While the manifesto of Anders Breivik was written in the context of a disparate international far right in the form of the counter-jihad movement, the Christchurch shooter's was written at the start of the decline of a broad, widely known movement in the form of the alt-right. Breivik's was long and tedious, largely copied from its highly disparate sources, and unlikely to convince anyone on its own. The Christchurch shooter's, by comparison, was an attempt to motivate would-be terrorists, already highly radicalised, to actually carry out attacks, couched in the parlance of existing internet memes. Neither was meant to convince, but the Christchurch shooter's in particular was meant mostly to incite.

SCRIPTED VIOLENCE

Although Breivik, the Christchurch shooter, and the El Paso shooter appeared as isolated figures, their ideas and actions were the product of both the swarm and more or less stable groups within the far right. Indeed, despite their attempts to distinguish themselves from these murderers, the media-savvy identitarians of the previous chapter are not entirely walled off from them. The framework of 'scripted violence' allows us to see the connections. A distinct voice – a far-right personality or group – identifies a problem, repeatedly using inflammatory and dehumanising language, and emphasises the absence of a conventional political solution. They rarely, if ever, tell their followers to commit acts of violence; however, their messages are read as such.

Far-right influencers are particularly prone to provoking scripted violence. Their focus on capturing and maintaining an audience rather than movement building creates a need for the escalation of language, and their lack of direct control of their followers allows for plausible deniability in the violence's aftermath. Their rhetorical recklessness is excused. The radicalisation of Darren Osborne, who killed a Muslim worshipper leaving Friday prayers in Islington by driving his van into a crowd, proves an extraordinarily neat example. In the space of a month, Osborne went from watching a BBC documentary about child sexual exploitation in Rotherham to murder. A fortnight before the attack, Osbourne started following far-right influencers, including Tommy Robinson, on social media. He received an email from Robinson describing Islam as 'a nation within a nation' that was 'built on violence and hatred.' Like the Christchurch shooter, he had also not radicalised on the more extreme platforms.

Movement-builders have to be more careful: their command over their members implicates them to a much greater extent. Scripted violence is a problem for identitarians who seek to sell themselves as conventional political actors with radical but not extreme ideas. Their movements come under sudden and unwelcome scrutiny in the wake of terroristic violence. After the Christchurch shootings, Generation Identity was placed under investigation by the Austrian state.

But the extent to which the far right is damaged by these attacks is highly dependent on the actions of other groups and the media in the aftermath. Immediately after the Christchurch shootings, the BBC saw fit to interview Generation Identity about their ideology and its connections to the murders. Even in the flimsy guise of a heavily hedged criticism, this explosion in audience reach accomplished more for the far right than years of metapolitical stunts had done. One way the metapolitical system of swarms, talking heads, conspiracies, and movement building that we have outlined above might come to an end is simply that BBC editors regularly place fascists on their shows.

SQUAD VIOLENCE

Squad violence is the output of those distinct groups that form among the blackpilled: in the UK, National Action, and in the US, most prominently Atomwaffen and The Base, although these are not the only examples.

National Action

National Action were a neo-Nazi group in the UK, which emerged in 2013 from the radical fringe of the BNP. After a few marches, which were successfully shut down by anti-fascists, they shifted to performing obviously racist stunts, like putting a banana on the statue of Nelson Mandela in central London. Unlike Generation Identity, they lacked the capacity to turn these stunts from media spectacle into a widespread popular discussion point. Their crassness and the openness of their Nazism prevented them from gaining wider traction. They were proscribed at the end of 2016 and one of their most prominent members, Jack Renshaw, was arrested for plotting to murder his local MP and inciting a child to engage in sexual activity. National Action were substantially modelled on Atomwaffen, and likewise had a presence on Iron March.

Atomwaffen

Atomwaffen continued the US tradition of intragroup murder: several of the many murders they collectively committed were of their own members. Influenced by a syncretic mix of extreme ideologies, their violence might be understood as the output of a group increasingly obsessed with its mystical power: dangerous, but not systematically so. Their propaganda itself is chaotic. One image posted on their website shows an armed member of Atomwaffen standing side by side with someone wearing the anti-Nazi Three Arrows symbol under the caption "we share the same fight against the system". Some of this is clearly trolling – an image from the same set states "We are with you Korea" in both Hangul and English, under an image of the North Korean flag. But much more is simply undecidable. The easy syncretism of violent ideologies makes clarity on these extreme groups not just difficult to achieve, but actively resisted.

The Base

Not all squad violence is so atomised or so apparently unplanned. Formed in July 2018, the international coalition of cells 'The Base' has attempted to move steadily towards planned attacks through a network of operatives who connect both locally, in person, and internationally, over the internet, to share resources. It taps into the deep wells of survivalism, prepping, and militia movements already extant in the US not just to plan for societal collapse but, as it fantasies, accelerate it. In all of these aspects it is similar to the earlier group Posse Comitatus, which started in the late 1960s.

The Base's leader, Rinaldo Nazzaro, understands it as a plausible future militant wing of something like the Northwest Territorial Front – a plan to secede the most north-westerly six states of the US from the country in order to found a white ethnostate. Its connections with Atomwaffen, then, lie mostly in their broadly similar aesthetics. This, however, is no small thing. The group attempted to carry out several major attacks on the US – one involving a shooting at gun rights rallies in a deliberate escalation of tensions between gun rights activists and the state – and ultimately failed in all of them. The problem might be located in the lack of discipline in the membership: seduced by the extreme aesthetics of the group, and imagining themselves to be entering into something like Atomwaffen, group members became more and more willing to carry out ill-judged attacks on their own. The Base was an attempt to reimpose a kind of hierarchy of command onto young people who had previously been uncommanded in their engagements with the alt-right. The more radical members of the group resisted this kind of control, turning towards planning more direct forms of violence, and as a result the group as a whole was cracked down on by the state.

Another factor that led to splintering was the group's hugely uneven texture of online and in-person contact. Nazzaro rarely appeared in person; he lived in Russia. Yet, new recruits were encouraged to meet up all the time; prizes were offered for those who posted their faces to the group's internal conversations. The unevenness of trust and rumour that this produced in the movement at large was almost certainly a factor in the major problems they later faced.

The Base, and the confusion and resistance caused by the re-imposition of command, might be understood as the turbulent consequence of the relation of multiple parts: the post-1983 White Power revolution in command, which took the name 'leaderless resistance'; the complicated relationship between commitment, intensity, duration, and command that characterised the alt-right; the relationship of the alt-right's distributed and open network to the necessary command structure and hierarchy of militant wings of separatist political movements and fascist movements more generally; and the complex blends of trust and rumour that characterised the uneven attempts to promote in-person meetups versus online propagandising.

Azov Battalion

Azov Battalion, a combatant in the ongoing conflict in Ukraine, has become an important node in the internationalisation of blackpilled violence. Here, after all, is real war, an ongoing violent conflict in which at least one side (the Ukrainian far right) seems sympathetic. This conflict functions similarly to the wars in Syria and Iraq for Islamic militants: they provide a training ground in which the far right can gain real conflict experience.

SECRECY

Far-right groups propagate conspiracies. But they themselves are not immune to conspiratorial explanation. The influence of O9A on Atomwaffen, or the intelligence services on the The Base, led to accusations from other neo-Nazis that both groups were honeypots set up to entrap prospective extremists. The Base's leader Rinaldo Nazzaro introduced himself on far-right podcasts as a former CIA operative, and was employed as an intelligence specialist. When it was revealed that he resided in Russia, these accusations of CIA involvement contorted into the possibility he was a Russian double agent. This combination of neo-Nazi, Islamist, Satanist, and other extremist ideologies, combined with the CIA and the Russian FSB, compressed through the encrypted and highly spoofable information channels of the internet, and situated in an ongoing geopolitical conflict, makes for a head-spinning conspiratorial blur.

Authenticity is a more general problem for groups on the edge of legality. Atomwaffen saw fit to disavow a video that showed members burning the Quran, the Tanakh, and (almost comically) Raymond Geuss' *The Idea of a Critical Theory*, as well as an LGBT flag, because it pointed towards an email address they denied was theirs. From then on, recordings of James Mason's voice became the stamp of authentic communication. This will, of course, not last: soon, voices and even videos will be just as spoofable as an email address.

This crisis of verification has not yet been resolved. Later, on 8kun, the replacement board for 8chan, one anonymous user posted a link to this disavowed video along with a bunch of links to Telegram channels. Who were they? A cop? Someone playing a prank? The replies refract confusion: "I love what you guys do, can I get a patch?", and another "Don't you feds have a tor website, too?", and another "Literally White ISIS."

THE FUTURE

It could be that the shootings of the last decade were an aberration. Or they represented another cycle of violence that has been, for now, brought to an end. But we could be faced with a more worrisome proposition. Climate change is coming down the pipe towards us. How might the blackpilled respond? In the next chapter, we address the justifications for killing that climate change might provide for would-be terrorists, and the wider transformations of the far right that the (so far, speculative) rise of ecofascism entails.

ECOFASCISM

Just because it's often been a fascist narrative, that doesn't mean that apocalyptic collapse *isn't* happening. Climate breakdown will be a source of enormous stress on the global economy, culture, and our collective life support systems. Millions of people will leave their homes to find safer places. Wars will almost certainly spread, and violence will become an increasingly major part of billions of people's lives worldwide. Some parts of the globe will become uninhabitable. If places such as Europe – where much of the far-right politics we have discussed comes from – will be sheltered from the worst of the immediate effects by virtue of their wealth, political power, and comparatively mild climates, the vast majority of people in Europe and North America will not be spared the sudden, unpredictable and irreversible contraction of their standards of living, as supply chains intermittently seize up and fall apart. Across the globe, in highly uneven ways, it will begin to look a lot like the end of the world.

If this seems alarmist, consider that the COVID-19 pandemic of 2020 was almost certainly the first of many, increasingly damaging, pandemics and other extreme climate events.[76] If climate change has often been imagined as a single great wave breaking over New York City, or a series of blazing hot summers, now is the time to face reality. Climate breakdown will not be a single event, but a series of highly complex stressors on society like the COVID-19 pandemic: stressed global supply chains; an unprecedented contraction and the detachment of millions of people from it; shelter-in-place orders; a rise in state intervention into life; emergency legislation; and global racialised finger-pointing. These waves of shock will be highly unpredictable, but their overall frequency and intensity is likely to increase. Like accelerating wave motion, eventually the pattern of social shocks will shift over into turbulence, and each crisis will become indistinct from the last, their effects rapidly spiralling beyond control.

As narratives of long-term material progress face their self-evident refutation and atrophy even further, people in Europe and North America will withdraw their support from industrial modernity and the liberal social order, and place it in whatever promises to extricate them from their predicament. Indeed, the struggle to articulate and explain the unfolding disaster of anthropogenic climate breakdown might well be the central challenge of political narrative-making in the 21st century and beyond. Why are we saying all this? In part, because the far right will almost certainly be positioned well to provide a compelling, if entirely false, narrative about both the breakdown's causes and its drastic solutions.

In the long term, this might coalesce into any number of movements and political formations that could be labelled in advance as 'ecofascism'. Under such circumstances, fascism might return, not only as a political form that relies on myths of civilisational rebirth, but also as a movement that melds together extreme and public violence with mass participation in the party or movement form. Indeed, what is perhaps so worrying about the relationship of fascism to the conditions created by climate change is how well they seem to fit together: the collapse of a 'natural order' through unstoppable and catastrophic 'decadent' growth seems to lead inexorably to the opportunity for a racist 'palingenetic' movement of national or civilisational rebirth. Fascism requires a sense of crisis, one that needs immense violence to prevent or reverse. Again, climate change, which seems insoluble within both the current economic system of capitalism and with the current geopolitical order of – as the far right sees it – compromise, hedging and mediocrity, might be just such a crisis.

CONTEMPORARY FAR-RIGHT ECOLOGISTS

There are multiple strands to far-right thinking about nature, which we can separate into three groups: the right-to-far-right political parties; a variety of movement-based identitarian approaches; and blackpilled collapsists.

The first group – from the New Ecology initiative of the French Rassemblement National to the coalition of the right-wing Austrian People's Party and the Green Party to the cynical use of the climate-like COVID-19 pandemic by the Fidesz government in Hungary – contains some parts that are explicitly strategising around our climate-breakdown future and some that will opportunistically push through their existing policies in times of crisis. Environmental politics have been alloyed with anti-immigrant and far-right policies in the Five Star Movement in Italy and have been cynically used by the US Center for Immigration Studies to promote anti-immigration policies. The deep institutional roots of these organisations and their ability to organise politics at the scale of the nation-state will likely make them key players in the early right response to climate breakdown. However, some of these parties have been embroiled in various ways for too long in the practice of climate denial, and their fundamental interest in maintaining a relatively conventional capitalist modernity will prevent them from taking what will increasingly seem like necessary action. In this they are likely to be understood from their right – in the long run – as simply another instance of the failed political centre. Their supporters will be up for grabs – and this could be an immensely important opportunity for the left. However, as they withdraw from these groups, these supporters will not automatically join the left-environmentalist movements, too committed to social justice for their tastes. Where will they go instead? Perhaps, rightwards.

The second group – movementists of the right and identitarians – are perhaps the most worrying group for the long term. Their main focus – cultural politics and its variations – is flexible enough to produce widespread hatred towards refugees, assuming these increase by virtue of climate change. Indeed, versions of far-right ecologism were adopted by the now-defunct Identitarian Movement UK and American Identity Movement. The latter summarised its connection with environmentalism in one of its sticker campaigns: "Plant trees, save the seas, deport refugees". These groups' organisational flexibility, and perhaps even more importantly their relative youth, which inoculates them from obvious accusations of blame for our future predicament, will let them thrive when the right and far-right parties look (by comparison) like increasingly sclerotic apologists for the liberal capitalist order. Political savvy and ability to translate smoothly between racist fears about migration and the spectacle of a declining natural order make this kind of movement the most serious threat. These political ideas proliferate on the internet and such groups have found common cause with the masculinist movement, as well as anti-modern currents more generally. Presently, these groups (at least their European variants) aim to influence the state, although depending on the success of their broader metapolitical strategy, they could come to be a serious alternative to the largely left-leaning mainstream climate movement.

The last group – the blackpilled collapsists – are banking not so much on a mass politics that turns the white populations in Europe and the US against people of colour as on a full-scale social collapse of order in which they plan to thrive – both personally and with their packs. They often deploy survivalist and prepping language and, in America at least, dovetail neatly with existing militia groups, whose concerns about infringement of gun rights can easily expand to include declining social and environmental stability. One of the most important cultural changes in the last few years, both on the far right and in the wider culture, although largely disparaged, is the mainstreaming of prepping. As unexpected breakdown events become more frequent, so the logic goes, so too does the rational case for preparing for them become stronger. In retrospect – writing from the inside of the COVID-19 pandemic – the turn of these blackpilled groups, such as international group The Base, towards recruiting from the ex-military wing of the US prepping scene seems like extraordinary foresight on their part. It goes without saying that their politics is less obviously attractive to masses of people at the present moment and, indeed, the numbers of far-right actors involved in such groups are smaller than the voting public of large far-right parties. However, this might not remain the case.

Climate breakdown, that long dark tunnel into which our planet is heading, has no clear solution, and neither do the distinctions between these three segments have much solidity. We said in the previous chapter that there is a tension between deadly violence and movement building. It may not always be so: the contradiction between the two is resolvable if the broader context changes. Widespread climate breakdown has the potential to be such a change. As the 21st century progresses, the currently stark distinction between identitarians and the blackpilled might start to wane.

In the context of global catastrophe, one central plank of anti-fascist strategy – pointing out the connections between movements and the terrorists they would attempt to disavow – might begin to be less effective. Consider the case of the shootings of migrants on the Greek/Turkish border in early 2020. Where before the violence of Greek fascists was treated as aberrant, when rumours that the migrants were infected with COVID-19 spread, the case for warding them off – using deadly violence if necessary – began to seem more reasonable for the far right.

The central argument of anti-fascist opposition to 'ecofascism' must be that it is not only likely to be politically catastrophic but also unlikely to solve the climate crisis itself. Indeed, despite the long history of environmental concern on the far right – from the conservationism of Madison Grant to the supposed 'green wing' of the Nazi party – the far right has extracted from the box of 'nature' a large number of distinct lessons; it has, in power, consistently worked to destroy the natural environment. Instead of a biocentrist defence of the sanctity of all life, what it has almost entirely been concerned with, through this history, is not nature but access to nature: preserving both a particular structure within nature and the social relations that allow people to access and engage with it. It is this we call 'far-right ecologism'.

Far-right ecologism is built around the attempt to stabilise and resolve a contradiction between two opposed conceptions of nature. On the one hand, nature is conceived of something true and eternal, whose ultimate triumph is guaranteed: nature is the central regulatory ideal of society. On the other hand, nature is almost always presented as something that has been obscured in fact. Thus, it must be restored by the deliberate and often extreme acts of its most ardent exemplars – often a particular race. On the one hand, nature is eternal and pure and irresistible. On the other, it has *always already inexplicably been resisted* by the far right's enemies. Attempting to resolve this underlying contradiction in the ideology of nature is the central task of far-right ecologism.

What does this have to do with capitalism? Perhaps such a contradiction simply indexes a deeper ambivalence in far-right politics: a wish to enjoy the spoils of capitalist expansion without the attendant social transformations that such a process has often entailed. Racial domination cannot be achieved without the operations of capitalism. However, capitalism also entails both ever-escalating production and resource extraction, destroying particular aspects of the life-world the far right wants to root itself in. Further, capitalism inexorably tends towards its own globalisation. Rootness (and its attendant social forms) is undercut by the force (capitalism) that gives that rootness its particular sense of its own superiority.

Our second book, *The Rise of Ecofascism* (Polity, 2022), will deal with these possibilities and dynamics. Here, however, the structure of the far right has been elaborated enough. We have attempted to clarify the relationships between all the various strands of the contemporary far right. It is now time to discuss how we can respond.

CONTEMPORARY ANTI-FASCISM

How do anti-fascists respond to all that we have discussed in this book: feelings and swarms, influencers and deadly violence, conspiracies and ecofascism? We have avoided prescriptions thus far. In fact, concrete prescriptions might be exactly what is *not* needed. As the far right continues to diversify, any single method of anti-fascism becomes inadequate. However, this fracturing amongst the far right also suggests a strategy of its own. Because the far right is not a singular entity but is filled with antagonisms and contradictions, anti-fascists should look to those antagonisms, apply pressure to them and break them apart.

The 21st century will be defined by ecological calamity. This must not be compounded by the political calamity of ecofascism. For this reason, anti-fascism needs to scale up dramatically over the next few years and decades. It will require patient and honest self-reflection to get there. We should therefore inspect the dynamics of anti-fascist movements now, in order to better prepare ourselves for the future.

Contemporary anti-fascism in the Global North – and we should emphasise again the particularity of our analysis of the far right to the Global North as well as the same geographical particularity of our remarks on anti-fascism – is unlike many of its historical forebears in three main ways. Firstly, it is unattached, usually, from party or state structures, although this is not the case everywhere. Secondly, the object of its attention is more diffuse, and consequently, thirdly, it must act across a variety of domains. These transformations, among others, have led to pronounced tensions in contemporary anti-fascist movements. We should attempt to understand these conflicts as directly emerging from specific features of anti-fascism as a *particular kind* of political organising and the contradictions and tensions it throws up.

THE SCOPE OF ANTI-FASCISM

There are two, caricatured, views of militant anti-fascism. We might call them the 'minimum' and the 'maximum'. The former has a narrow focus: it involves exclusively direct action against expressly fascist organisations. At the latter, anti-fascism becomes identical to broader left organising. The argument for the latter goes: the suppression, once and for all, of fascism, would be a consequence of the left achieving all its other goals. Because fascism is so intimately related to the ongoing reproduction of capitalism, anti-fascists can scarcely treat it as separate.

These two positions are not simply different-size versions of the same thing. The maximum does not straightforwardly contain the minimum. If the maximum could be achieved and anti-fascism became a sufficiently diffused component of leftist organising as a whole, the minimum would no longer be as necessary – it would, at the very least, be transformed into something else. The idea that scaling anti-fascism to its maximum means producing simply a *bigger* version of the minimum has produced a great deal of confusion.

Instead, scaling anti-fascism will require rethinking and reconstructing, attending to its multiple necessary functions, not least of which is the development of networks of critical engagement and care. It will require organisations capable of relating to the wider left, to the communities in which the far right organises and to those communities most at danger of far-right violence. It will, at moments, require clandestinity. It will, at moments, require direct confrontation with the far right, on the streets, where they attempt to assert themselves. But it will not be exclusively focused there.

This is not a call for this 'maximum'. Neither it nor the 'minimum' are ever realised for long. The minimum, indeed, is never reached, because its apparent laser-focus obfuscates the distributed and often gendered networks of care that go into making it. It runs up against the state and against the problem of its own organisational reproduction. Meanwhile, the maximum is also beset by problems of its own organisational reproduction: in attempting to deal consummately with the phenomena of fascism, it can tend towards its own prematurity, exhaustion, diffuseness, platitudinousness.

There are concrete goals shared by both the minimum and maximum, of course, which are more or less unarguable: that fascists are rendered unable to act, organise, recruit, or form organisations; that the left is free to carry out its activity without fear of physical attack; and that oppressed groups and other minorities can lead their lives untroubled by fascist violence. But beyond this, what anti-fascism requires is both an openness to new strategies and an openness to the critique of strategy.

If the picture of the far right in this book holds, then the question anti-fascists ask themselves must change from "who are the fascists?" to "how is fascism forming itself out of the disparate parts of the far-right movements that currently exist?" Or even, "who or what is making the world more conducive to fascism?" Claims that something is worth anti-fascists opposing should be made *on these grounds,* and in terms of these questions. Much like 'the left' and 'communism' (or whatever utopia it aims at) can be distinguished, one can distinguish between 'fascists' and 'fascism', and the distinction is useful for understanding the immense circuitousness and ineptness of much action by the far right and fascists. There are plenty of fascists, for example, who are doing almost nothing to make the world more conducive to fascism. Indeed, they may be doing exactly the opposite.

'DIVERSITY OF TACTICS'

To combat the far right's spread, we variously use techniques: research into and breaking up far-right groups as they form; deplatforming; deradicalisation; assisting people with constructing a leftist view of the world; and 'counter-speech' or counter-demonstrations. Each of these can be applied at different points, and each has a cost. Each tactic works in conjunction with the others, but anti-fascist organisations that attempt to leap immediately to doing all of them will exhaust themselves quickly.

Population-level susceptibility to the ideas of the far right is also highly dependent on economic and other crises, as well as the degree of novelty and salience of the particular formulation of the far right in question. It is the struggle to change this susceptibility itself that we describe as 'maximum' anti-fascism: to address the multifaceted crises of capitalism to which fascism responds, and in doing so to attempt to undermine the ease with which fascists can gather force. This is why we say it is identical with the left, but those transformations go beyond these more focused interventions detailed here.

Research and breaking up far-right groups as they form

The strategy we have already hinted at is the production of tensions between far-right groups. It goes on underground, and is perhaps principally responsible for what is known as the 'prevention paradox'. The reason there has been no return to fascism at the scale of the 1930s is partially down to the ever-vigilance of anti-fascists at this level, below its most public moments. Research of this kind involves piecing together the concrete networks of the far right and exerting pressure on key individuals, as well as persuading those on the outskirts of networks that the costs of being publicly exposed are too high ('doxxing').

Far-right organisations are beset by new tensions and contradictions particular to the internet. Whereas once far-right organisations were rigidly hierarchical, the hypertrophied growth of their propagandistic functions has destabilised this. Those in the group who are technically 'in charge' are not always those who produce the most or the most popular content. Tensions between these two parts of the organisation can sometimes be exploited and personal acrimony made to thrive.

Deplatforming

In the UK after World War Two, fascist activists, many of whom had been interned during the war, exploited resentments in deprived communities in order to rebuild their shattered politics. The 43 Group – made up largely of

Jewish ex-servicemen – returned from what they understood as a war against fascism to find it being preached on the streets. In response, they adopted a famous and spectacular tactic: they would rush the back of crowds at fascist rallies in a wedge formation, pushing through it and tipping over the very literal 'platform' on which a speaker was standing. Such was the birth of 'deplatforming'.

Today, the logic of deplatforming has shifted. On the internet there is a proliferation of ways to speak and be heard. If one of the main ways fascism is made more likely is through the densification of far-right networks, then one of the main tasks of anti-fascists is to disrupt them. Can the swarm's platform be tipped over? The answer is no. But this doesn't mean anti-fascists are helpless, or that no-platforming has come to an end. The swarm is not an undifferentiated network but often forms around highly connected nodes: far-right influencers, whose power and vulnerability comes from their significantly more exposed position. By deplatforming these figureheads, the swarm's capacity for coalescence, and therefore organisational reproduction, is reduced. For online far-right movements, experiencing content within a community is what sustains engagement with a movement. Remove it, and the community begins to wither. Bluntly: it has to be made less fun to be in the far right online. Although ejection from the main platforms is damaging to far-right figureheads, their disappearance does not mean they become irrelevant. Deplatformed influencers still form part of the tapestry of guest hosts, contributors and chat participants that provide frisson to online far-right activity. Anti-fascism here is not unlike hydra-slaying: the allied pages of a banned Facebook group revive it as a new head with minor modulations.

Unlike in the days of the 43 Group, the internet is made up of many platforms. Some, like Parler, Gab, DLive, and Bitchute, have been set up specifically as 'free speech' sites with much looser rules on hate speech. Others, like Telegram, are less concerned with active moderation. It has become standard for influencers to set themselves up on alternative platforms or, as in the case of Mark Collett, strictly tailor content to particular platforms' terms of service, and really let loose elsewhere. Influencers anticipate their eventual deplatforming and develop contingencies that are communicated well in advance. Some of their audience (those over whom they hold most sway) will follow them to these alternate platforms. These are likely to be the most radical, and they enter a new network often shorn of its moderating influences. This is a substantial risk to the strategy: suppression of a far-right group can produce a smaller, more radical group of fascists, who in turn produce the blackpilled. However, left alone, the problem simply worsens. Groups allowed to grow will produce more blackpilled people – when they are, of necessity, opposed – than smaller groups.

There are additional differences from the anti-fascism of the post-war moment. Now, fascists are removed from platforms not through direct anti-fascist action but through the often unexplained decisions of corporate owners. Facebook, Twitter and TikTok are operated for shareholder value. They are more than willing to remove fascist accounts if that value is threatened. Or, for that matter, anti-fascist ones. In mid-2020, a slew of anti-fascist accounts were banned from Facebook under a revised interpretation of their terms of service. Online, at times, the push for deplatforming has harmed anti-fascist capacities.

The far right is also assailed, at times, by the state. In the UK, two far-right organisations – National Action (and their derivatives) and Sonnenkrieg Division – have been proscribed, a legal process that prohibits being a member of an organisation as well as expressing support for them. For anti-fascists, proscription is insufficient. Like the axing of far-right social media accounts, these interventions cut both ways – leftists are also persecuted by the same state.

Deradicalisation and reradicalisation

The next two interventions come as a pair: deradicalisation, the process of 'treatment', is supplemented by the further step of reradicalisation. Far-right activists frequently separate themselves from others and their social isolation often makes them more susceptible to joining the far right in the first place. However, once they get more deeply involved, they are obliged to spread their message. It is here that the toolkit of 'everyday anti-fascism' becomes useful: making interventions into the process of drifting towards the far right, preventing susceptible people from being dragged towards the far right, and preventing those would-be radicalising people from reaching others.

At times, fascism can understand itself as a critical ideology: it sees through the liberalism that others seem to accept without thought. This is, of course, a characterisation we would dispute. As we have repeatedly said, fascism is the radicalisation of the deeply conventional racist and sexist logics that undergird our modernity. But something in this appearance of radicalism can be useful. For this reason, reradicalisation – the process of transforming people from far-right activists to leftists – might perhaps be easier than the process of deradicalisation considered on its own, where far-right politics is replaced with the absence of politics. For this to happen, the left needs to appear to those being deradicalised not as the dupes of capitalism, but as a more radical critique. This is why our analysis here has emphasised that, for the most part, the far right aim at the continuation of the status quo by other means. The actual overthrow of the world's brutal pattern of governing separations requires a leftist analysis.

'Counter-speech'

By the same token, 'counter-speech', a tactic largely proposed by centrist NGOs in which people enter far-right spaces online and propose other views of the world, can be effective as long as it offers something more than 'not hating people'. Technological versions of the same, such as Twitter's new features – prompting you automatically to rethink your slur-filled post – are probably justly derided.

Those with a more potent view of the world can offer more. In one particularly effective example, the streamer Hasan Piker and the host of the Three Arrows YouTube channel spent three hours talking round a Jordan Peterson fan who was at high risk for further radicalisation. It is not for nothing that Contrapoints is one of the most widely cited instigators of a moment of realisation for those deradicalised from the alt-right. Other strategies, such as Joshua Citarella's long-game strategy for Instagram, which takes advantage of the dense private networks of group chats that prop up political posting's often baffling front-end to slowly shift people's ideas, are equally useful.

Street anti-fascism and the production of anti-fascist organisations

Anti-fascists often appear on the streets, to oppose the movements the far right spews forth. Although the preceding chapters make it clear that's not the whole of the far right, and of course this isn't the whole of anti-fascism, it's still the most obvious and visible part. So, how are these anti-fascist street manifestations to be arranged, announced, coordinated? And then on the day, how are the marchers to be kept safe until everyone is home again? How is the reproductive work that goes into sustaining the well-being of anti-fascists, work that usually falls *ad hoc* to women and non-binary people, to be coordinated more justly? And finally, how do anti-fascists sustain themselves as a coherent political movement *between* actions?

Anti-fascist organisations are a response to a requirement that emerges not from some abstract political imperative, but from the actual structure of anti-fascism itself: there must be a coordinating organisation. The risks associated with political action in the street are compounded when anti-fascist movements are divided. These organisations largely have a territory they are responsible for: a city, a town, an area of a country. As such, they must be alive and responsive to the complex and conflicting demands of the people who live in that area, as well as to people most vulnerable to far-right violence. They must, in short, be democratic in the richest sense of the term, which means they must also be aware of the limits of their own decision-making powers. They therefore need to be continually in conversation with the wider left, for whom fascism forms a shared enemy. Indeed, for the left, the need to construct a coordinating organisation for anti-fascism is supported by anti-fascism becoming a component of all forms of leftist organisation.

Democracy does not mean everything is out in the open. Anti-fascism contains an element of clandestinity. But this clandestinity, and the pressures inherent therein, means mistrust can quickly spread throughout a movement, and as such these organisations can sometimes degrade into smaller groups, which then compete with one another for exclusive control of an area. The arrhythmia of anti-fascism is unhelpful. Anti-fascists frequently have little to do that is particularly appealing (although, as you can see, there is always more research to be done), yet organisational exclusivity compels strong identification with the cause among the group's members: 'if *we and only we* are the anti-fascists, then we need to be *doing antifascism* even when it's not obvious what that is.' No longer do anti-fascists ask 'who can help us all to best mobilise against the threat of fascism?', but 'who is the exemplary anti-fascist?' and therefore, 'how can others be shown not to be?' With exemplarity comes hubris, the feeling of ownership and an aversion to risk.

In this logic, both the failures and successes of others become suspicious: failure because it shows they were never the right kind of anti-fascist, for surely the 'correct kind of anti-fascists' would succeed; and success because anti-fascism is necessarily coalitional and therefore comes at the price of alliances with 'bad actors', however these are designated. We should be honest that just as the ideal fascist – obnoxious, easy to spot, coherently incoherent, clearly within a particular historical lineage of the far-right – is mostly a fiction, so too is the ideal anti-fascist – radical, committed, ideologically pure, and involved in a network that is itself also exclusively radical, committed, and ideologically pure.

Linked to this imaginary clash of ideal fascists and ideal anti-fascists is the terrifying ballooning of the supposed threat from fascism. As the pool of sufficiently ideal anti-fascists shrinks, so their enemies seem to multiply. We have said that fascism's wide scope of concern is parasitic on the increasing depth of capitalism's command of life. This breadth can make fascist attitudes seem to be multiplying. While it's true that the far right remains a substantial threat to the left globally and attempts to downplay their influence almost always fail to take account of the prevention paradox discussed above, it is not true that fascism is everywhere. Similarly, the logic of anti-fascism cannot simply be straightforwardly applied to other targets. Anti-fascism is the not the general process of distinguishing the pure from the impure, the right from the wrong, or the safe from the dangerous. Anti-fascism is not the security wing of the left, yet it is also not as simple, as we have repeatedly stated, as drawing a boundary around the people with swastika tattoos on their faces.

These two poles – the need for a singular organisation to coordinate action and the demand for ideological purity – are in an animating tension that can spiral into mudslinging and social schisming. Solving this dilemma isn't a matter of asserting the absolute primacy of one over the other. But a rejection of purism provides a corrective to this tension. By virtue of its organisational exclusivity, anti-fascism demands openness to all potential comrades.

It can do so by making itself not just a political organisation but also a cultural form – a metapolitics (deliberate this time) of the left. What might this mean, now that the corpse of punk has finally fully dissolved? Anti-fascism has sometimes traded on an image of what we called earlier 'minimum' anti-fascism – blackblocked, righteous young people, involved in scenes of chaos with a transparently *evil* enemy. This riot aesthetic, like the 'stunt' aesthetic discussed in chapter 8, is almost *excessively* potent on social media. It circulates freely as a set of spectacular images. It's *fucking cool* when it's not cringe. Yet it is obviously insufficient as a cultural form; it invites approval and outrage, but not participation.

Subculture has often been anti-fascism's crutch. It provides an element of vibrancy, of just enough stuff happening to give a movement life. But it is also a limiting factor. The group of people who would be anti-fascists have nothing in common culturally, which is perhaps how it should be. The challenge, then, is to imagine what anti-fascist culture might become, not as something that grafts itself on to an existing set of cultural objects – a particular kind of music, meme, or political argot – but as a diverse culture in its own right. In wider society, belonging to a particular social group is no longer a matter of shared aesthetic tastes anyway. Much as watching content online forms part of the organisational reproduction of the far right, so the organisation of anti-fascism, open to its own multifaceted articulation, might become its own self-sustaining kind of cultural form, capable of bringing people in at scale.

And what would be the content? A turn away from a culture founded on particular cultural objects does not mean that organised anti-fascism should make itself mute on all matters other than fascism. It is also, as another wing of this same strategy, necessary for anti-fascism to engage with contested cultural spaces that are productive of fascists. Where is this kind of contested cultural space at the moment? As noted in the previous chapter, in the future it will be largely in the response to climate change. Right now, it is also tied up in the much larger anti-racist movements to which anti-fascism currently plays a junior role.

Such movements, most prominently Black Lives Matter, draw the ire and often the violence of the far right. This is one reason that anti-fascists should be interested in said movements, but more important is that anti-racist movements challenge anti-fascism's abritary cut-off point for engaging with racism. When 'minimum' anti-fascism fails to recognise the continuity between racism and gendered violence in wider society and the racism and gendered violence of the far right, it falls back into dogmatic conceptions of what it is trying to oppose, relying on its own memory of the last unambiguously far-right movement, and thus always lagging some years behind changes in the actual far right. Simultaneously, by distinguishing itself absolutely from anti-racist movements, 'minimum' anti-fascism fails to substantively address the underlying causes of what it is attempting to oppose.

At the same time, not all the tactics of anti-fascism are appropriate or even useful against broader structural racism. You can't deplatform centuries of colonial violence. The solution, we tentatively suggest, is to resist the process of exclusive identity-formation that goes into joining or being a member of anti-fascist organisations; to resist the process of self-mythologisation without denying the genuine heroism of much anti-fascist activity; and to, wherever possible, support and involve oneself in the broader process of dismantling structural forms of racism.

ANTI-ECOFASCISM: ANTI-FASCISM AT SCALE

In the previous chapter we discussed the emergence of far-right responses to the impending climate crisis. Anti-ecofascism will have to be organised on different scales, and will have to respond to the specific conditions of each scale – that of states and political parties, movementist ecofascism and blackpilled collapsism. The scale that is likely to be the most susceptible to conventional tactics of anti-fascism is that of movementist ecofascism. This is because the identitarian-style movements likely to form the bedrock of this part of ecofascism are already here, and already facing opposition from anti-fascists in multiple countries. This of course does not mean that anti-fascists should ignore state authoritarianism, which has historically been one of the key components of the fascist formation.

One needs three aspects to be able to understand the arrival of fascism: the state's prior gathering of authoritarian instruments, the development of radical movements that contest the state's power at its points of contradiction, and the context of widespread complex crises. Such a multifaceted concept of fascism might seem to make opposing fascism confusing. But, on the contrary, it can also mean that the struggle against fascism emerging in the future is also the struggle against milder forms of authoritarianism emerging now.

ANTI-FASCISM AND UTOPIA

What is anti-fascism's utopia? It is perhaps almost entirely negative. Anti-fascism aims for a world free of the possibility of fascism. But if fascism is understandable as the systematisation of capitalism's governance through racism, sexism and class domination, then anti-fascism's wish for a world free of the possibility of fascism is a world free of these altogether. All three are inextricably bound up with the rule of capital. The ultimate anti-fascist goal – a world free of the possibility of fascism – is thus a world that has transcended capitalism entirely.

POSTSCRIPT: BEYOND TRUMP

The purpose of this postscript is to consider the events of 6th January 2021 and to attend to some of the sources of rising authoritarianism to which this book, being focused on the far right, has perahps not paid sufficient attention.

The storming of the US Capitol on the 6th January 2021 scandalised the libs.[77] Some journalists declared it a coup. Others denounced those journalists as hand-wringing alarmists, cynically enabling a power grab by increasingly authoritarian centrists in the Democrat party. The riot was portrayed by liberals and some anti-Trump conservatives alike as proof of the finally-revealed insurrectionary truth of Trumpism. Thereafter, Trump could be placed conclusively *beyond politics* and into the bipartisan realm of national security threats, more akin to a terrorist than a president. QAnon's bizarre beliefs were useful for this project of making Trump seem exceptional. They seemed to want to live in an entirely different world. It was a small step from there to to seperating them from the rest of society. Order restored.

The riot also seemed – briefly – to have triggered the long-awaited detonation in the faultline between Trump and the 'moderate' Republican party, but it wasn't to last. Despite some strong statements in the wake of the riot, Republicans quickly fell back in line, not so much to Trump himself but to his loyal core constituency. A proposed bipartisan commission into the riot failed to attract the necessary Republican votes.

Liberals are very keen to regard the Trump period as a strange pause in the otherwise untarnished post-Civil Rights history of the US. Despite the mass still following him, some analyists continued to try and split Trump off from the rest of politics, to treat him as an excisable pathology and not a symptom of a deeper problem. What are the stakes of this attempted exceptionalisation and containment of Trump? What might it mean for us – boldly, 'the left' – to insist instead on Trump's continuity with the rest of that history? Ought we to? The question, particularly for anti-fascists, requires a nuanced answer. Anti-fascism is clearly supportive of related processes of exceptionalisation; the idea that there is something specifically dangerous about fascism is in the name, but the ideas that that thing can be contained, or understood as distinct from the society it preys upon, is more contentious.

There are a few possible positions for anti-fascists to take: "this was fascism"; "fascism is possible but this wasn't it"; and "we shouldn't talk of fascism but *fascisation*, a process that spreads out over the social whole, consuming social relations bit by bit, a process in which this riot was an unmistakable uptick."[78] Which should we pick? First, let's see what model everyone else has chosen.

The rioters stood little chance of success. The characterisation of the riot as a 'coup' obscures some of the chaotic energy of the day – the scenes in the Senate chamber have the feeling of an uninspiring student occupation. To be sure, the rally had been planned, largely on message boards like thedonald.win, and other online platforms where QAnons congregated. Trump's order that the crowd head to the Capitol was probably deliberate instigation. Yet in the footage, it is clear that the rioters can't quite believe that they are getting away with it. This was no military assault. But we should not simply think that this was not fascism because it was not well-organised. There is nevertheless a more important point about the misapprehension of the state, one of the core objects of fascist politics. Even if they had been vastly more effective, what could the occupiers have achieved? The Capitol building is a mere symbol: occupying it even for months at a time would do as much to stall the workings of the state as would occupying a stock exchange stall the workings of capitalism.

Yet they were presented as halting the entire process of government, as seriously impeding the operations of the state. Both the riot itself and this framing of it point to constitutive fantasies shared by QAnon and liberals alike. Both seem to believe, falsely, that the state is localised in one place, or one person, or in one set of processes that are vulnerable to being overthrown by a single switch. For both, this switch is Trump. Consequently, both also believe that the far right is a threat to the existing order of things. They, therefore, seem to believe in the first possibility we outlined above: "this was fascism", or for QAnon, who would not use that word about themselves, "this was something absolutely distinct from the rest of politics, a moment of cleansing justice".

In truth, the far right and their beliefs are integral to the present order, and QAnon marks the moment of their still-deeper integration. QAnon, as we have already mentioned, is the culmination of the spread of authoritarian impulses in internet conspiracy cultures. While obviously not a component of the state, that was QAnon's constitutive fantasy. QAnon influencers regularly invoked their personal connections to 'military intelligence'. Those on the conspiratorial right, who were once most sceptical of the state's power, terrified of 'martial law', now imagined themselves its truest allies. All the baroque intricacies of the worldview – time travel, the hagiographies of Nikola Tesla, the Barron Trump mythology – are mere elaborations of this basic authoritarian fantasy. Because this fantasy made political activity largely redundant, QAnon's authoritarianism incurred passivity. Conspiracies are already the hallmark of those who do not know what to do politically, but in QAnon it became a self-reinforcing process. Endless instructions to 'trust the plan' reduced the need to actually do much.

What, then, explains the 6th January? Partially the fact that Trump had invited people to assemble. Partially, QAnon's hybridisation with other more active far-right tendencies. Resurgent militia and patriot movements, the OathKeepers, the Proud Boys, and so on, were all more committed to action than most adherents to QAnon. It is perhaps this ongoing hybridisation that hints at more worrying forms of far-right activity in the future. Yet, these groups, too, understood the state as a localisable entity that could be seized, contained perhaps within the briefcases of votes sent into the Congress.

Yet, below the level of symbolic opposition to a symbolic process, real politics continued to happen. What real politics? It rapidly became evident that the main consequence of the Capitol riot would be a reassertion of control by the security state in the US, most of all the FBI, now directly and explicitly supported in their work by liberal Twitter vigilantes scouring the internet for the faces of rioters.

Who, then, won from the Trump era? Above all, the security state. It secured the enthusiastic support of those who had been most sceptical of them: the conspiracy culture of Alex Jones et al. and the liberal establishment alike. In the first few months of 2021, the US Department of Homeland Security issued four separate warnings of domestic extremism. None materialised. The success of fascists has always been dependent on the prior accumulation of authoritarian instruments by the conservative state. The contemporary far right exists in a complex dance with the rising authoritarian powers of increasingly brittle neoliberal states, but so too do its liberal defenders. This fascisation process proceeds not just in the Capitol riot but in the security state's response to it, and amongst the liberals cheering it on.

But anti-fascists are concerned with fascism. What does this inexorable expansion of the security state, especially when it seems so *internal* to the liberal order, have to do with us?

Here we must question and broaden our idea of the far right. Politics is the struggle to produce or reproduce a set of social roles and relations. Our definition of 'far right' locates a particular position within this struggle. More a taxonomic family than a species, we define it as 'those forms of political behaviour that work on or advocate for the reproduction of capitalist social roles and relations on the basis of ethnic nationalism, racism, xenophobia or antisemitism, and often through the application of violent means at odds with principles of formal equality and thus at least publicly unavailable to the liberal state'. Because of its generality, 'the far right' doesn't have one particular organising form. Indeed, a case could be made that the most important far-right political actor in the Cold War, for its role in crushing left-wing dissent worldwide, was the CIA. In this sense, 'the far right' appears not as a distinct thing from the organisation of capitalism, but as its 'bleeding edge', more in continuity with the 'prerogative state' of interwar fascism than with its street movements.

It is in this context that we can address the exceptionalisation and containment of Trump. It is important to understand the events of 6th January as a process of fascisation. Trump represents a break from the past, but a break that emerges from a well-integrated fraction of the existing order: its authoritarian and brutalising forms, its degradations of democracy, its deep stratifications by race and gender. He represents an acceleration of the process of fascisation, not its fully achieved form.

Was the 6th January a victory for the far right? It remains to be seen. What it unquestionably did, however, was strengthen authoritarian impulses *whether they come from the far right or the centre*. It is this subtle, but important transformation in the structure of politics as a whole, and its benefit to *any* future fascist movement that will be the most important consequence for anti-fascists in the future.

It is not restricted to the US. In the UK, the right-wing Conservative government has accelerated the decades-long accumulation of authoritarian instruments, recently tabling even more police powers over public protest through the Policing, Crime, Sentencing and Courts Bill.[79] In France, laws passed by Emmanuele Macron banned the filming of on-duty police. In India, the Modi government cracked down on dissent using 'anti-national' laws. In Brazil, activists were murdered by paramilitaries, both in the police and out of it.

It is perhaps not just fascism proper that needs opposing, but the fascising process as a whole, the slow violence of deepening all the brutal and inegalitarian parts of social relations.

And, so, what next for 'anti-fascism'? How have the threats to the left changed in the post-Trump era? How will the events of the 6th January be configured in the centrist authoritarianism of the future? What use might be made of the spectre of 'fascism' by this politics? And what does this 'state anti-fascism' have to do with anti-fascism proper?

These are questions not for a book, but for a movement.

NOTES

INTRODUCTION

---

1. The favourite maxim of Andrew Breitbart of Breitbart News.

2. This distinction rests in part on Saull, Richard, Alexander Anievas, Neil Davidson, and Adam Fabry. '*The Longue Durée of the Far-Right: An Introduction*'. In Longue Durée of the Far-Right: An International Historical Sociology. Routledge Studies in Modern History 14. Abingdon, Oxon; New York, NY: Routledge, 2015.

FASCIST FEELINGS

---

3. The collection of common ideas, images, and rudimentary thoughts a group articulates in its politics.

4. Han, Byung-Chul. *The Burnout Society*. Translated by Erik Butler. Stanford, California: Stanford Briefs, an imprint of Stanford University Press, 2015. p. 35-51

5. Paramilitary units famous for killing Communists in Weimar Germany, some of whom went on to form the Nazi party.

6. Theweleit, Klaus. *Male Fantasies Volume 1: Women Floods Bodies History*. Minneapolis: University of Minnesota Press, 1987, p. 46.

7. A UK-based far-right street movement. See Chapter 6, 'The Street'.

8. A famous atheist, a far-right influencer, and the flag of the fictional alt-right nation 'Kekistan'.

9. A letter of the proto-Germanic alphabet used as a symbol by ecofascists (see chapter 9, 'Deadly Violence') and a pan-European Identitarian group (see chapter 7, 'New Organisational Forms').

10. See chapter 6, 'The Street'.

11. See chapter 8, 'Deadly Violence'.

12. A UK-based blackpilled group, and a US-based one, respectively. See chapter 8, 'Deadly Violence'.

13. Crumplar, Mike. 'Blissful Beginnings: Elliot Rodger's Sexual Awakening'. Mcrumps Blog (blog), 7 January 2020. https://mcrumps.com/2020/01/07/blissful-beginnings-elliot-rodgers-sexual-awakening/.

14. Collett, Mark. *The Jewish Role in the Porn Industry*. https://www.bitchute.com/video/AsHhUdvPtHpY/. See chapter 7, 'New Organisational Forms'.

15. See Chapter 8, 'Deadly Violence'.

16. Chu, Andrea Long. *Females*. London; New York: Verso Books, 2019.

17. A UK-based street movement. For discussion of similar movements, see chapter 6, 'The Street'.

18. Horkheimer, Max, and Theodor W. Adorno. *Dialectic of Enlightenment: Philosophical Fragments.* Edited by Gunzelin Schmid Noerr. Translated by Edmund Jephcott. Cultural Memory in the Present. Stanford, Calif: Stanford University Press, 2002. p. 143

METAPOLITICS AND AESTHETICS

19. Anti-Defamation League. *'Computerized Networks of Hate'.* New York; Anti-Defamation League, 1985. http://archive.org/details/ComputerizedNetworksOfHate.

20. Swain, Carol M., and Russell Nieli, eds. *Contemporary Voices of White Nationalism in America.* Cambridge, UK ; New York: Cambridge University Press, 2003, p. 154

21. See chapter 6, 'The Street'.

22. Friberg, Daniel. *The Real Right Returns: A Handbook for the True Opposition.*

23. This tension between the highly organising thinking of the right's intellectuals and the incoherent grifting of their more popular mouthpieces will be the subject of chapter 6 on The Right's Intellectuals.

24. Collett, Mark, and No White Guilt. *Patriotic Weekly Review - with Jared Taylor.* Accessed 28 November 2020. https://www.bitchute.com/video/z4xM7mT-q30/.

25. Hawley, George. *Making Sense of the Alt-Right.* New York: Columbia University Press, 2017. p. 56

26. Friberg, Daniel. *The Real Right Returns: A Handbook for the True Opposition.*

27. Soules, Marshall. *Media, Persuasion and Propaganda.* Edinburgh University Press, 2015. https://www.jstor.org/stable/10.3366/j.ctt1g09zzm. p. 132

28. A right-wing YouTube alternative.

29. A point Mann, Michael, *Fascists*, p.3, makes, although the concept has been much over-stretched here and elsewhere. See Davies, Christie. 'Goffman's Concept of the Total Institution: Criticisms and Revisions'. *Human Studies* 12, no. 1–2 (June 1989): 77–95. https://doi.org/10.1007/BF00142840.

30. Ganesh, Bharath. 'The Ungovernability of Digital Hate Culture'. *Journal of International Affairs* 71, no. 2 (2018): 30–49.

31. Greenwald, Glenn. 'How Covert Agents Infiltrate the Internet to Manipulate, Deceive, and Destroy Reputations'. *The Intercept* (blog), 24 February 2014. https://theintercept.com/2014/02/24/jtrig-manipulation/.

32. Gogarty, Larne Abse. *'Coherence and Complicity: On the Wholeness of Post-Internet Aesthetics'.* BAK, basis voor actuele kunst, 2018. https://vimeo.com/266048660.

33. See Chapter 4, 'The Swarm and Influencer'.

34. See Chapter 8, 'Deadly Violence'.

CONSPIRACY THEORY

---

35. Wilson, Andrew. '#whitegenocide, the Alt-Right and Conspiracy Theory: How Secrecy and Suspicion Contributed to the Mainstreaming of Hate'. S*ecrecy and Society* 1, no. 2 Secrecy and Authoritarianism (16 February 2018), p. 10

36. Dunn, Tom Newton. 'Ex-British Intelligence Officers Say Jeremy Corbyn Is at the Centre of a Hard-Left Extremist Network'. *The Sun.* 7 December 2019. https://web.archive.org/web/20191207145207/https://www.thesun.co.uk/news/10501848/jeremy-corbyn-extremist-network/.

37. Boltanski, Luc. *Mysteries and Conspiracies: Detective Stories, Spy Novels and the Making of Modern Societies.* English edition. Cambridge, UK: Polity Press, 2014. P. xvi

38. Sacasas, L. M. 'Narrative Collapse'. *The Convivial Society* (blog). Accessed 1 August 2020. https://theconvivialsociety.substack.com/p/narrative-collapse.

39. Schuetze, Christopher F. 'Germany Shuts Down Far-Right Clubs That Deny the Modern State'. *The New York Times*, 19 March 2020, sec. World. https://www.nytimes.com/2020/03/19/world/europe/germany-reich-citizens-ban.html.

40. Stoddard, Lothrop. *The Rising Tide of Color Against White World-Supremacy.* Honolulu: University Press of the Pacific, 2003.

41. Grant, Madison. *The Passing of the Great Race: Color Illustrated Edition with Original Maps.* Eastford, CT: Martino Fine Books, 2017.

42. The term Renaud Camus, one of the theory's most important progenitors, uses, in direct translation.

43. Lane, David. 'White Genocide Manifesto', 1 October 2019. https://web.archive.org/web/20191001213058/https://www.davidlane1488.com/whitegenocide.html.

44. See Chapter 8, 'Deadly Violence'.

45. Postone, Moishe. 'Anti-Semitism and National Socialism: Notes on the German Reaction to "Holocaust"'. *New German Critique,* no. 19 (1980): 97. https://doi.org/10.2307/487974. P. 106

46. Mann, Michael. *Fascists*. Cambridge; New York: Cambridge University Press, 2004. P. 27

47. Horkheimer, Max, and Theodor W. Adorno. *Dialectic of Enlightenment: Philosophical Fragments*. Edited by Gunzelin Schmid Noerr. Translated by Edmund Jephcott. Cultural Memory in the Present. Stanford, Calif: Stanford University Press, 2002 p. 173

48. Ibid p. 140

49. Barkun, Michael. *A Culture of Conspiracy: Apocalyptic Visions in Contemporary America*. Comparative Studies in Religion and Society 15. Berkeley, Calif: University of California Press, 2003. P. 6

THE SWARM AND THE INFLUENCER

50. Hawley, George. *Making Sense of the Alt-Right*. New York: Columbia University Press, 2017. p. 70

51. Han, Byung-Chul. *In the Swarm: Digital Prospects*. Untimely Meditations. Cambridge, MA: MIT Press, 2017. p. 11

52. Tuters, Marc. 'LARPing & Liberal Tears: Irony, Belief and Idiocy in the Deep Vernacular Web'. In *Post-Digital Cultures of the Far Right: Online Actions and Offline Consequences in Europe and the US*, edited by Maik Fielitz and Nick Thurston.

53. See Chapter 8, 'Deadly Violence'.

54. Trilling, Daniel. 'Tommy Robinson and the Far Right's New Playbook'. *The Guardian*. 25 October 2018. https://www.theguardian.com/world/2018/oct/25/tommy-robinson-and-the-far-rights-new-playbook.

55. We discuss Patriotic Alternative in more detail in our chapter on New Organisational Forms.

THE RIGHT'S INTELLECTUALS

56. Mann, Michael. *Fascists*. Cambridge ; New York: Cambridge University Press, 2004. p.8

57. Sedgwick, Mark J., ed. *Key Thinkers of the Radical Right: Behind the New Threat to Liberal Democracy*. New York, NY: Oxford University Press, 2019.

58. See Chapter 8, 'Deadly Violence'.

59. Bronze Age Pervert. *Bronze Age Mindset*. Independently published, 2018.

60. Donovan, Jack. *The Way of Men*. First Edition. Dissonant Hum, 2012.

61. Carrère, Emmanuel. *Limonov*. Translated by John Lambert. London, England: Allen Lane, 2014.

62. Tait, Joshua. 'Mencius Moldbug and Neoreaction'. In *Key Thinkers of the Radical Right: Behind the New Threat to Liberal Democracy,* edited by Mark J. Sedgwick. New York, NY: Oxford University Press, 2019 p. 195

THE STREET

63. Groups of fans of a football club which form part of 'hooligan culture'.

64. VICE News Tonight. *Charlottesville: Race and Terror.* Documentary, 2017.

NEW ORGANISATIONAL FORMS

65. See Chapter 2, 'Metapolitics'.

66. A conservative pressure group in the UK.

67. Belew, Kathleen. *Bring the War Home: The White Power Movement and Paramilitary America.* Cambridge, Massachusetts: Harvard University Press, 2018.

DEADLY VIOLENCE

68. Broszat, Martin. *The Hitler State: The Foundation and Development of the Internal Structure of the Third Reich.* London ; New York: Routledge, 1981.

69. Institute for Economics and Peace. 'Global Terrorism Index 2019'. Accessed 14 January 2020. http://visionofhumanity.org/app/uploads/2019/11/GTI-2019web.pdf, p. 34- 49.

70. Ebner, Julia. *The Rage: The Vicious Circle of Islamist and Far-Right Extremism.* London: I.B. Tauris & Co. Ltd, 2017.

71. Césaire, Aimé. *Discourse on Colonialism.* New York: Monthly Review Press, 2000.

72. Gallagher, Sean. 'Breaking the Law: How 8chan (or "8kun") Got (Briefly) Back Online'. Ars Technica, 11 May 2019. https://arstechnica.com/information-technology/2019/11/breaking-the-law-how-8chan-or-8kun-got-briefly-back-online/.

73. We have approximated this naming convention from the official report into the attacks: 'Royal Commission of Inquiry into the terrorist attack on Christchurch masjidain on 15 March 2019', which refers to him as 'the individual'.

74. The original is 'access to history even at the price of destruction', from Arendt, Hannah. *The Origins of Totalitarianism*. New ed. A Harvest Book HB244. New York: Harcourt Brace Jovanovich, 1973. P. 332

75. Arendt, Hannah. *The Origins of Totalitarianism*. New ed. A Harvest Book HB244. New York: Harcourt Brace Jovanovich, 1973. p.183

ECOFASCISM

---

76. Pandemics are an example of an environmental crisis because the zoonotic transfer which sparks them is often a consequence of rapid destruction of animal's natural habitats.

POSTSCRIPT: BEYOND TRUMP

---

77. Liberals, especially those on Twitter.

78. See Palheta, Ugo. 'Fascism, Fascisation, Antifascism'. *Historical Materialism,* 7 January 2021. https://www.historicalmaterialism. org/blog/fascism-fascisation-antifascism.

79. See NetPol. 'EXPLAINER: What Does the New Policing Bill Say about Restricting Protests?' *Netpol,* 13 April 2021. https:// netpol.org/2021/04/13/explainer-what-does-the-new-policing-bill-say-about-restricting-protests.

12 RULES FOR WHAT

----

12 Rules for WHAT is a podcast and writing project about the far right, hosted by Sam Moore and Alex Roberts. Their second book, *The Rise of Ecofascism*, will be available in early 2022 from Polity Press.

@12rulesforwhat   12rulesforwhat@protonmail.com

WANT SOME STUDIO

Want Some Studio is award winning illustrator Marco Bevilacqua. Marco creates detailed hand drawn pencil illustrations that incorporate portraits, typography and wee icons. The work is usually created with a range of fancy pens and pencils, some £1.00 felt tip pens from Lidl and a wee bit of digital from his studio in Edinburgh, Scotland.

wantsome.studio

DOG SECTION PRESS

Dog Section Press is a not-for-profit publisher and distributor of seditious literature, and a registered worker-owned cooperative.

dogsection.org

Other titles from Dog Section Press:

Abolishing The Police
Various Authors

Great Anarchists
Ruth Kinna and Clifford Harper

Animal Squat
Double Why

Make Rojava Green Again
Internationalist Commune of Rojava

The Rhyming Guide to Grenfell Britain
Potent Whisper

NO! Against Adult Supremacy
Stinney Distro

Subvertising Manual
Brandalism

Subvertising
Hogre

Advertising Shits in Your Head
Anon.

Options for dealing with squatting
Persons Unknown

Forthcoming titles from Dog Section Press:

Revenge
Clifford Harper

Social Ecology and the Rojava Revolution
Various Authors

DOPE Anthology (1-10)
Various Authors

Black Anarchism
Zoe Samudzi

DOPE

MAGAZINE

DOPE Magazine is a quarterly newspaper published by Dog Section Press. Through a horizontal network of distributors around the UK, people ranging from rough sleepers to asylum seekers can collect copies for free, sell them for the cover price of £3 and keep the full proceeds.

DOPE is also free to prisoners, who can request a subscription via Haven Distribution.

Help us to get more DOPE Magazine to more people in more places by supporting our Patreon.

patreon.com/dopemag
dogsection.org/solidarity

DOG SECTION PRESS